PN 1991.55 .H28 1991
Halper, Donna L.
Radio music directing

occOR Jan-30-1995 10:41

DATE DUE			

Radio Music Directing

ELECTRONIC MEDIA GUIDES

Radio Music Directing

Donna L. Halper

Focal Press
Boston London

Focal Press is an imprint of Butterworth–Heinemann.

Library of Congress Cataloging-in-Publication Data
Halper, Donna L.
    Radio music directing / by Donna Halper
            p.   cm. —(Electronic media guide)

    ISBN 0-240-80081-8
    1. Radio programs, Musical—Planning.   2. Radio music directors.
    3. Radio—Production and direction.   4. Radio broadcasting—United
    States—History   I. Title. II. Series.
    PN1991.55. H28 1991
    791.44'0236—dc20

                                                    90-43785
                                                    CIP

British Library Cataloguing in Publication Data
Halper, Donna
        Radio music directing.—(Electronic media guide)
        1. Radio programmes. Production. –Manuals
        I. Title II. Series
        791.440232

        ISBN 0-240-80081-8

Butterworth–Heinemann
80 Montvale Avenue
Stoneham, MA 02180

10 9 8 7 6 5 4 3 2 1

Printed in the United States of America

I definitely get by with a little help from my friends. The people who helped me with this book are too numerous to mention, but a special thank you to the ever patient staff at the Curry College Library. Thanks also to Mike Keith, Gerry Brenner, Phil Quartararo, Michael Plen, Bruce Schoen, Tom Jodka, Mike Symonds, Joe Ianello, Sheila Chlanda, Tom Kay, Bobby Poe, and all the other good folks in the music industry who have stood by me over the years. And a salute to Jefferson Kaye, Dick Summer, Bruce Bradley, and Arnie Ginsburg, who inspired me to get into radio and who exemplify the best of what an "air personality" can be. Thanks also to my husband and best friend Jon Jacobik, who never once complained about how much time this project took. And, last but not least, thanks to God, who has never forgotten me.

Contents

Preface

According to common wisdom, there are two basic types of radio listeners: *actives* and *passives*. The latter are people who like music and enjoy listening to it, but who listen to radio as sort of a background activity. They tend not to call the station to enter a contest, nor do they notice when the announcer gives the wrong birthdate for a certain artist or plays the same song that was just played three hours ago. Passives don't make a study out of radio, and they don't take it seriously. They just know what they like, and once they find it, they tend to stay. Actives, however, treat radio as a foreground activity. They listen closely. They know that the announcer messed up on that rock star's birthdate and, yes, they will call and correct the misinformation. Actives make lots of requests, and get tired of songs quickly. While they like the hits, they also like to hear new songs. Actives will sample as many stations as they need to in order to find something interesting. And once they do find it, they leave as soon as it gets boring. But when actives do find a station that meets their needs, they are vocal about it and extremely loyal.

Most of the people I knew while I was growing up were passive about radio. They had a favorite station or a favorite song, but radio wasn't their life. And, as these things usually go, I was an active. I didn't know back then that there was a name for people like me, radio-junkie that I was. I just knew that without my transistor radio, I felt incomplete. I didn't mind that Top-40 stations repeated the same songs: I loved rock, and the late 1950s were still a very experimental time for pop music. I remember once when I was sick in bed and home from school, waiting patiently for my favorite station's Hot Rotation to recycle so I could hear "Peggy Sue" by Buddy Holly one more time. When there were contests, particularly music trivia, I always knew the answer; but by the time I called, it seemed they already had a winner (or the line was busy). But I kept on trying, even though I seldom, if ever, got through. I knew all the words to all the songs: when I was lonely, Top-40 comforted me, and when I was happy, Top-40 expressed my mood. Like many kids my age, I felt my parents and teachers didn't understand me, but unlike some of them, I never rebelled through doing drugs or quitting school, and to this day, I have never even tried alcohol. Rather, my rebellion took the form of a career choice: at a time when there were no women on the air except for an occasional cooking show, I decided I wanted to be a disc jockey. It was difficult to overcome the sexism of the times, but finally, in 1968, I did my first show, becoming the first women DJ at Northeastern University.

It was at my college station that I discovered the job of music director (MD). Up until I learned what went on behind the scenes, I had always assumed the announcers picked the music. When I found out that program directors and MDs did that, I knew I had found exactly what I wanted to do. It was so much fun that I continued to music direct at some very respectable major-market stations, including WMMS in Cleveland, WRVR in New York, WAVA in Washington, D.C., and WHDH in Boston. By being a music director, I was also able to have great influence on the careers of numerous groups, most notably *Rush*, whom I discovered while at WMMS; they dedicated their first two albums to me. I loved working as an MD, and for a long time, even after I became a program director and then a consultant, I wanted to write about what MDs do and how the position has changed over the years. Now, thanks to Focal Press, I am finally able to tell the story of some very important but often overlooked people: music directors.

Acknowledgments

Special thanks for their willingness to be interviewed for this book to: Lenny Beer, Bob Clayton, Marge Bush, Joel Denver, David Farrell, Larry Douglas, Juggy Gayles, Brian Interland, Mike Harrison, Kemosabi Joe, Larry LeBlanc, Dennis O'Malley, Mel Phillips, Bobby Poe, Kal Rudman, Jim Smith, Ed Salamon, Smokey Smith, Ed Shane, Dave Sholin, Dick Summer, Rosalie Trombley, Charlie Parker, Mike Sigman, and Bob Wilson.

Also, thanks to Tim Powell for the interesting recollections of the early days of AOR, and to Chris Golden of *Billboard* for the facsimile of *Billboard*'s first issue from 1894.

1

The Roots of Music Directing

Music director. Some people have never heard of the position, while others assume it has to do with symphony orchestras. Yet, in radio, the job of the music director is one of great importance. The title itself is relatively recent, but the task of selecting the right music at radio stations has been ongoing since the early 1920s. Radio's music directors (MDs) are often unsung heroes, launching careers and helping songs become hits. It's a challenging job: obviously, with so many records being released each month, not all of them *can* be hits, and even the ones that music directors truly believe in are not always meant to succeed. Good music directors have to know what fits their station's sound, as well as what songs have hit potential. In this book, we will explore in depth just what a radio station today expects from a music director—what the job entails, how it has evolved, and some helpful tips on how to be a success at it.

No job ever seems to appear out of nowhere, and music director is no exception. In order to fully understand what a music director does, some history is in order. For those of you who dislike history, read on: you'll find that what we currently think is so modern and unique to our times can actually be traced back to the 1890s! True, there weren't any radio stations back then, but of course there was music . . . And where there was music, there was also business. Middle-class culture in the 1890s placed great importance on being able to play an instrument (piano was especially popular). And, since there were no movies or video games or radio stations, one of the most frequently enjoyed activities was gathering at someone's home to sing. It didn't matter if you had a good voice or not; communal sings were an enjoyable way to socialize. And what did people sing? Yes, even then, there were *hit songs*, although what we today call a *hit* is based on record sales and airplay, which of course was not possible back then. The hits of those days came from a variety of sources, some more socially acceptable than others. On the one hand, among the socially correct were well-known poems set to music, as well as songs first performed in plays or operas. There were also traveling musical troupes, called *singing families*, who went from town to town entertaining audiences with the newest songs. Immigrants were arriving in large numbers, and they too provided popular songs, many of which had originally been the folk music of their country. On the other hand, there were songs that evolved from the taverns and barrooms. Most upper-class people condemned these songs as vulgar, and probably a few were. But we should also remember that the American national anthem, "The Star Spangled Banner," written by Francis Scott Key, was set to music in 1814, using the melody of a well-known British drinking song.

Meanwhile, what would eventually become the music industry that we know today was getting started in that era around the turn of the century. Since so many people enjoyed singing, they needed to know the words to their favorite songs. And in 1900, the way to accomplish that was to buy the sheet music. Printing words and music was not a new idea: in the early 1700s, psalms had been set to music and then printed up for use in churches. By the late 1700s, at least one entrepreneur, Benjamin Carr, had opened a music publishing firm that sold sheet music—even in those days, popular songs existed, and although there wasn't yet a huge demand, there was enough to keep Mr. Carr's company busy. By the mid 1800s, songwriting had become a profession, rather than just a hobby (and a poor hobby at that: the legendary composer Stephen Foster was only paid $100 for one of his most famous songs, "Oh Susannah"), and the demand for lyrics to songs continued to grow. Benjamin Carr had been ahead of his time, but his efforts to print up and sell sheet music led to other companies entering the business.

By the 1890s, there was a thriving group of songwriters and sheet music publishers working in New York City; the area around Union Square where they all worked came to be called *Tin Pan Alley*. There are several versions of how this name was chosen, one of which credits the name to songwriter Harry von Tilzer, while the other claims music publisher Monroe Rosenfeld thought it up. Either way, the name resulted from the fact that on any hot summer night in the 1890s, all the songwriters kept their office windows open and a pedestrian walking through Union Square would hear a cacophony of off-key pianos from those songwriters trying to write their next hit. Harry von Tilzer once told a reporter how the noise that resulted from all those pianos, which were often played one-finger style, reminded him of "kitchen clatter, just like tin pans." The description worked: Tin Pan Alley was born.

Up until then, songwriters received little respect. Some sheet music publishers refused to put the composer's name anywhere in sight, and, as mentioned earlier, songwriters weren't paid much, no matter how many copies of the sheet music were sold. All this, however, changed with the ever-increasing demand for new songs. While the critics dismissed popular music as overly sentimental and poorly written (and, of course, inferior to "good music," such as classical or opera), the public wanted more and more. Popular songs provided the average person with a way to forget life's daily problems, which is still the main reason there are hits even now. Today's audiences may be more sophisticated or have more labor-saving devices, but the same subjects that struck a responsive chord for the fans of the 1890s (losing one's only true love, feeling misunderstood, worrying about the future) are still being turned into No. 1 songs a full century later.

The songwriters, who were mostly male, quickly realized that the buyers of sheet music were mostly female. Out of this emerged perhaps the first *target audience* (a market research term that refers to a specific group at whom a particular product is being directed—the target audience for acne medication, for example, is teenagers). In the music industry's formative years, the female role was clearly defined. Women were expected to be the guardians of the home, imparting proper social values (piety, chastity, hard work) and living up to an idealized image of motherhood. Part of that image involved knowing how to play piano and teaching her children music. Thus, songwriters began composing songs they felt would appeal to these dedicated housewives, for the more women liked a song, the more they would want to own the sheet music. Songwriters had become adept at seizing upon topics that would reach large numbers of people: during wartime, they composed patriotic tunes as well as laments about mothers whose sons had died for their country. During peacetime, if a hot issue such as women's suffrage arose, or if a new invention such as the automobile was making an impact, songs and sheet music quickly appeared. And of course, they always wrote plenty of love songs. The public seemed to like tearjerkers, and several songwriting teams became known for their ability to make the audience reach for the handkerchiefs.

In addition to songwriters becoming better paid and more appreciated, another aspect of the music industry that we still see today was taking hold. People wanted to be entertained, and those who considered themselves middle class enjoyed going to a nice place to hear the new songs performed. Such respectable venues as Tony Pastor's Music Hall and the Union Square Theatre gave the genre known as *vaudeville* a better image. At one time, vaudeville had been considered lower class; the entertainers even told jokes that no decent woman of the 1890s should hear. But the new vaudeville theaters featured family oriented shows, with not a hint of impropriety. They also featured another growing phenomenon: celebrity singers. Of course, these stars didn't attract the attention or adulation that today's rock stars do, but it became very obvious to members of Tin Pan Alley that a song's popularity, as well as its sheet music sales, could be greatly enhanced by having a famous singer perform it. Sheet music, meanwhile, had changed from dull to artistic: most sheet music of the 1890s featured beautiful and ornate cover pages. Needless to say, it didn't take long before certain songs became associated with certain performers, whose pictures appeared on the sheet music.

Also in the 1890s, Thomas Edison was doing experiments that would later change the entire music business. As early as 1877, he had found a way to record the human voice, and by the 1890s, a few adventuresome classical musicians were making phonograph records. Few people owned phonographs, and it would be many more years before record sales would have an impact on whether a song became a hit, but the music industry that we know today was gradually taking shape. Edison would also make another contribution with the invention of moving pictures, as we will discuss later.

The turn of the century was an exciting and creative time. More new publishers went into business; more songwriters were working. Everyone seemed to prosper, and the public was delighted. This was also a time of dance crazes. Like singing, dancing was considered a socially acceptable pastime, although the preference was for serious and stately dances like the waltz. Suddenly, in the 1890s, a new up-tempo dance, *the cakewalk*, became the newest fad. Immediately, Tin Pan Alley was there to provide music to do the cakewalk to. This soon became a trend: whatever the new fad, there would be new songs and sheet music about it, thus making that fad even more popular. But how could the writers and publishers take an even more active role in shaping the public's tastes? Then, as now, the answer was *promotion*. To those of us familiar with marketing and advertising, promoting a product is part of that plan by which the product attains first preference with the potential buyer. Today, we turn on the radio or TV and are immediately confronted with a number of clever messages intended to make us think of a certain chewing gum or car or perfume. But in the days before radio and TV, promoting was more of a challenge. As you know, phonograph records were not yet widely available, and even those people who did have a phonograph found the quality rather primitive. What had to be promoted to the average person of that era were *songs*, and the vehicle was sheet music.

As noted earlier, by the 1890s, there was a thriving music publishing industry, and intense competition. So, how could a publisher's songs get that ll-important top-of-the-mind awareness when so many songwriters were working overtime turning out a seemingly endless number of would-be hits? How could these songs get to the right people, namely the famous singers and band leaders? As today, popular music is spread by radio airplay, so in the 1890s, songs were spread by those vaudeville performers, some of whom still traveled to major cities throughout the United States. It was no accident when performers added certain songs to their repertoire. Part of this process occurred because some well-known songwriters had achieved a reputation for being able to write a song that people would like; thus, performers sought out these successful songwriters to see what their latest compositions sounded like, and if the song sounded right, a sale was made. But the rest of the process involved some behind-the-scenes work. Not every performer has time to go around to every songwriter. Also, some of the newer songwriters had not yet had enough hits to win the trust of the biggest stars, who knew even then that the wrong material could hurt their careers.

At first, the publishers themselves made the rounds of the vaudeville theaters, bringing with them songs they wanted the performers to use. It could be a time-consuming job: Edward Marks and his partner Joseph Stern divided the task, but they still had *100* theaters between the two of them to visit *each week*. Needless to say, that didn't leave either of them much time to write or to solicit new songs they might want to publish. And it wasn't as simple as paying the performers a visit: the publishers had to actually perform each song so the performers could get an idea of how it sounded, and then the publishers would attempt to persuade the performers of each song's great hit potential. (This, by the way, is not that far removed from what the record promoters of today have to do to get their songs played on radio; they may not sing the songs, but they do play them and then try to convince the program directors and music directors that they are listening to the next No. 1 smash hit. More on this later.) It didn't take long for experienced publishers to see just how competitive Tin Pan Alley was becoming, and soon, just singing the songs for performers wasn't enough to get their attention. Soon, publishers were adding their own special touch to the way they introduced their songs.

In their excellent history of sheet music, *I Hear America Singing* (Crown, 1989), Lynn Wenzel and Carol Binkowski describe what promotion in the 1890s looked like.

> Publishers [had] a systematic formula that was at the heart of Tin Pan Alley. [They] became their own 'pluggers.' A plugger, originally called a 'boomer,' was a combined advance man, advertising czar, con artist, and entertainer. Julie Witmark, E.B. Marks, Charles K. Harris, and Joseph Stern, among others, led a very colorful life. [They] went from variety house to theater to restaurant to burlesque show, bribing orchestras with drinks, greeting performers, giving out

free song sheets, offering singers a percentage of profits on sheet-music sales, promising star pictures on sheet-music covers, and standing up and singing an extra chorus when their own song was on the bill. All this was to get their songs played more frequently.

So, it seems that what we know today as *payola* can be traced as far back as the 1890s, although certainly on a smaller scale. Singers were given free meals, royalties and their name on the song as a co-writer (although they didn't really write the song), and even gifts became a part of the plan: to make sure a song wasn't forgotten, some of the more prosperous publishers would give performers race horses or even boats in exchange for frequent and enthusiastic performances.

By 1900, music publishers were too busy to do their own plugging, so they hired people to do it for them. Some went on to become famous in their own right: the legendary songwriter Irving Berlin started his career as a song plugger for Harry von Tilzer's publishing company. Good song pluggers had to be charming; they had to be able to sing, dance, tell jokes, and o whatever it took to get the attention of the famous stars. Then, as now, having a major celebrity singing your song could ensure its success. When Harry von Tilzer worked as a song plugger, he wrote an article about it in a popular magazine of the day, and he described his work like this: "I'm a song promoter. I'm the man who makes the popular songs popular. I earn big money and I've grown into a necessity to the music publishing house that employs me. The company works one big town at a time. It sends on, by freight, a stack of the [sheet] music of the song to be made popular. It is not put on sale until I give the word." He went on to explain how by bribing the orchestra and practicing the song with them before the actual show, he arranged ahead of time, for his song to just happen to be played that night. Upon hearing it, he would then jump up, seemingly in a spontaneous burst of excitement, and start singing the song loudly, encouraging the audience to sing along. He had even hired someone to sit in the audience and begin to whistle the chorus, to further familiarize everyone with the tune. By these techniques, the song was promoted. (This and other interesting stories about early song plugging come from David Jasen's book, *Tin Pan Alley: The Composers, The Songs, The Performers, And Their Times.*) The custom of using "plants," people who were paid to sit in the audience and appear to be ordinary patrons until a certain song was played, at which time they would suddenly leap to their feet and sing (or applaud, whistle, him, or whatever else it took to create enthusiasm), became a common method of promoting. So did singing a given song in music shops, department stores, restaurants, or anywhere else the plugger saw a crowd. The intent was to get people to sing along, after which they would certainly seek out the sheet music, and another hit was born. Pluggers also used some show-business techniques: if they were promoting a song about a farm, they might dress up as farmers and drive around town in a hay wagon, singing the song. A song about bananas might entail hiring a trained chimp to do tricks or hand out bananas while the plugger displayed the sheet music for the crowd. Whatever it took to attract that all-important attention, the song pluggers would do it. This was understandable in a time where records were few and radio wasn't around yet. If live performances were the only way people could hear potential hits, then pluggers were ready to make their songs stand out. At times, especially by the standards of today, song pluggers may have looked ridiculous, but the turn of the century was a more innocent time, and many people found them amusing if not entertaining. It was definitely not a good job for anyone suffering from shyness.

If we want to look at the origins of music directing, perhaps the song pluggers were both promoters and directors. True, they had a vested interest in their own material getting performed, but it was they who were responsible for putting singer and song together and bringing the song before the public, be it at a dance hall or in a vaudeville theater. Meanwhile, enterprising music publishers were still seeking new ways to call attention to their newest songs. Thanks to Edison's work with moving pictures, there were soon viewing rooms being set up so that people could watch actual images amazingly projected onto a screen. The motion pictures of the 1890s were only a minute or two in length, and were seen in *penny arcades*: for one cent, a customer could look into a viewing machine, turn a crank, and see dancers, acrobats, animals, or perhaps an entire parade. While only one person at a time could use the machine, still, music publishers saw another opportunity to promote songs. Spoken dialogue in motion pictures was still years off, but background music for these new movies was very much a possibility. Edward Marks, already a successful songwriter and publisher, came up with an idea that combined song plugging with watching a movie in the penny arcade. This innovation was the illustrated song slide, which he put into use in 1895; it was an immediate success. Song slides starred the famous singers of the day, photographed in poses and scenarios that acted out the words to their latest hit. These dramatic poses made it easy for a viewer to follow along with the song and even understand the words better: perhaps song slides were the forerunners of music videos. It didn't take long for the vaudeville theaters to get involved too; they would use the song slides during intermission at their shows. The theater manager would project a slide on the screen and then a house vocalist would sing the song. Or, as you may have expected, a song plugger or a plant would suddenly provide the vocals and encourage the audience to join in. Once again, the listening public had been exposed to a new song, and with any luck, that song would soon become requested at other vaudeville shows, and the sheet music would begin to sell. Another hit had been made.

As you will see in upcoming chapters, what we do today to turn songs into hits is not that much different from what was done 100 years ago. The major difference between then and now, certainly, is radio airplay. But other than that, the basic premise remains the same: music publishers (today, managers of groups along with record companies) hire song pluggers (today, record promoters and publicists) to persuade singers and band leaders (today, program directors, music directors, and consultants) to perform a particular song often (today, play the song in frequent rotation on the radio). Back then, success was measured by sheet music sales. Today, hits can be determined from many configurations: records, cassettes, compact discs, 12-inch dance mixes, and even music videos, all of which can sell enough copies to ensure both song and artist of hit status.

The wise program and music directors today are aware of the latest trends and they have some familiarity with where these trends originated. For example, what is this quote talking about? "[We feel certain that] its days are numbered. We are sorry to think that anyone should have imagined this music was of [any] importance. It was a popular wave that went in the wrong direction."

Of course, you say, another old critic who hates rock and roll. That's a good guess, and it does sound remarkably like what the critics did say when rock was new. But no, this quote comes from *1901*, and the magazine article in question is about that vulgar new music the young people liked . . . Ragtime. Why did ragtime inspire such contempt from the critics? Partly because it wasn't considered "serious" music, like opera or the classics, ragtime had earned a bad reputation among music scholars and professors who felt young people should only listen to music that was educational. But another more likely reason for their dislike of ragtime was its roots in Black music. Just as the society of the early 1900s had rigid roles for women, so, unfortunately, was the society segregated in many ways. For example, as popular as vaudeville theater was, black performers were seldom if ever invited to perform there. Rather, they were restricted to black vaudeville theaters, where they were also paid less. Further, when whites performed certain songs, called *coon songs*, they would blacken their faces with cork and pretend they were "typical" blacks. I put the word "typical" in quotes because by our standards, the coon songs were incredibly racist, portraying blacks as simple, stupid, and laughable. Yet, proper white society found these coon songs entertaining and didn't seem to understand how stereotyped and offensive they would be for blacks. Since whites didn't usually attend theater performances with blacks, evidently the subject never came up for discussion, and coon songs continued to be written and performed. So, it was especially ironic that many whites still found themselves attracted to the music of black musicians. You may ask, if the society were implicitly segregated, where would whites hear black music? Some men heard it at the so-called sporting houses, a polite name for houses of prostitution that sprung up in certain cities. These sporting houses, which were in black neighborhoods, offered men a place to play pool, hear live music, and drink in addition to meeting a lady of the evening. The clientele was mainly black, but many whites became regular customers (until the houses were shut down by the police). Still, although a decent man couldn't admit to his wife that he had been to a sporting house and heard some great music (which, unlikely as it may seem, was one reason these places were so popular), the fact remains that many whites were first introduced to black musical forms by way of sporting houses.

Ragtime was another basically up-tempo style of music, in an era that was known for ballroom dancing, considered proper because it required gracefulness; ragtime dancing was accused of being lewd and suggestive because it necessitated a lot more body movement. Critics thus felt that doing such an immoral dance would undermine the values of middle-class polite society; a similar accusation would be leveled at rock music in the 1950s.

Consider the marketing challenge, though: here we have an era where blacks and whites aren't supposed to mix, women are supposed to be homemakers only, morality is clearly defined, and decent people only do dances like the waltz. It's the early 1900s, and your mission as a marketer is to make ragtime acceptable. Your challenge, of course, includes the fact that you can't admit that the place most men first heard it was in a house of prostitution. It also includes the fact that your target audience for sheet music purchases is made up of conservative women. Add to this another problem: ragtime was a complex music that required great manual dexterity and musical skill to play well on the piano. The average amateur would have a difficult time making ragtime sound good. And, in an era where songs had to have lyrics that touched the emotions, ragtime was instrumental. So, could you have taken on the job and turned ragtime into a hit with whites? It somehow happened, against all odds. One man who was responsible for making ragtime popular with whites was a southern white musician, Ben Harney. Harney had heard lots of ragtime in his native Louisville, Kentucky, and he had great respect for the black musicians who played it. He committed himself to learning to play it as well as they, and gradually, he succeeded. By the time he and his wife moved to New York, he had earned a reputation for his skill with ragtime. Playing regularly at the finest vaudeville theaters, Ben Harney exposed large numbers of whites to rags. The audiences were so impressed with this new music that it became a major fad. And where there was a fad there was Tin Pan Alley, which immediately began turning out songs with "Rag" in the title, in addition to writing some actual ragtime tunes for people to play at home. There were also some excellent black composers who did achieve some degree of recognition for their work in ragtime. The best known of these is Scott Joplin, whose songs have been adapted for plays and even used as movie themes. His best-known song was "Maple Leaf Rag."

But let's return to trend watching. Dance crazes like the cakewalk and musical crazes like ragtime stirred up controversy, as we noted earlier. Perhaps critics found these fads dangerous because they came from the streets, the black clubs, the sporting houses, and burlesque shows (before vaudeville became respectable, its more profane form was called burlesque, and it was aimed mainly at male audiences). This made these fads lower class, and hence, unfit for decent people. But then as now, the more the critics wrote against these fads, the more popular they became, especially with young people. (We will see the 1990s version of this in the rap music debate, in an upcoming chapter, proving once again that the more things change, the more they stay the same.)

Like it or not, ragtime prospered. Classical musicians were horrified, and they feared they would lose their jobs; one union, the American Federation of Musicians, took action in 1901, forbidding union members from playing ragtime anywhere. But, as you have probably noticed, the more you ban something, the more you make it attractive, even to those who are simply curious. In fact, rather than suppressing ragtime, the opposite occurred: even more fads arose, including some new dances that made the cakewalk seem tame. By 1912, the popular new dances were up-tempo, and to do them, dancers had to be willing to get out on the floor and actually shake their bodies. Being proper no longer mattered, nor did being graceful. Dancing was *fun*, and people were eager to participate. Again, it was in so-called lower-class establishments that the new dances began, but they spread rapidly to the middle class. Some of the new dances had amusing names: the Turkey Trot, Bunny Hug, Possum Trot, and Grizzly Bear (the so-called *Animal Dances*) were among the most popular. The tango also became a part of any good dancer's repertoire. But the new dances weren't without their detractors. Church leaders were vocal in their opposition to the new dances, which they regarded as sinful because certain of the dance steps required couples to dance close together or even hug on the dance floor (this was an era when public displays of affection were still frowned upon). Further, in some ways the dances were the forerunners of feminist sensibilities: no longer was the female the passive partner, led and guided by the man, as in the traditional waltz and other ballroom dances. In the new dances, the woman moved around just as freely as the man. This too prompted writers and clerics to predict society's ruin unless people returned to the old traditional ways of dancing. But, alas, this was not to be. For the average person, the fact that these dances may have evolved from black roots or in sporting houses was of no concern. Dancing was a fine way to pass time and make new friends. The young people couldn't understand why their elders were so upset. (Years later, similar outrage to that leveled at the Bunny Hug and Turkey Trot would be heaped upon the Twist, and other supposedly obscene dances of the 1960s.)

Once again, music proved to have a very positive effect on most people, and Tin Pan Alley was right there to meet the great demand for music to dance to. Ironically, despite the fears of the critics who condemned this music repeatedly, society as a whole seems to have benefited from the dance craze. Restaurants had to build dance floors. Hotels added ballrooms. More Americans were leaving the family piano and going out for an evening of dancing. And since there was still no radio (and not many dance songs on records yet), this meant the establishments had to hire dance bands. Some of these bands had black musicians, and soon, white audiences were flocking to see them. Not only did the growing popularity of dancing give many talented black musicians their first exposure before white audiences, but it also caused a boom in jobs for dance instructors. From about 1912 till the start of World War I, dancing schools sprung up in many cities, as people tried to learn the new steps so they would look good when they went to the dance hall. The music publishers were ecstatic: now, sheet music had a wider audience, not just women who stayed home with their children. In fact, the music publishing industry was doing so well that some all-black firms opened, and the coon song met its much-needed demise, replaced by a more respectful attitude about such black forms of music as ragtime, and later, jazz.

By now, you may wonder what's so important about dace crazes and music publishers in 1914. By itself, it's certainly just more history, but taken in context, it has a special significance: in order to fully understand how the music industry came to be so influential, it's instructive to follow how the industry grew and how the society around it was changing. For example, around this time, phonograph records were becoming more popular. There may have been only two major record companies (Victor Talking Machine and Columbia Gramophone), and the phonograph was an awkward-looking device with a huge horn and a crank; but gradually, recorded music was gaining credibility. Few people expected recorded music to replace live performances, but even then, people wanted to hear certain songs more than once. Records made that possible. By 1917, a popular patriotic song, "Over There," written to rally Americans during World War I, sold over two million copies of sheet music, and then, made an even bigger impact when legendary opera star Enrico Caruso decided to record the song; it became a big seller, one of the biggest of its time. Soon other big-name singers were recording patriotic songs with equally good results. Records also had another use: since there still was no such thing as hearing the hits on your favorite station, the next best way to practice the new dance steps was to buy records. There was also one other somewhat dubious trend that kept records popular. While the coon song had gradually fallen into disfavor with the establishments whose successful bands often had black musicians, some people still wanted to hear these songs and found them amusing for reasons that most of us today would find difficult to understand. Several record companies continued to record and market coon songs, and for those people who wanted to hear this type of music, records became the only way to do so.

When World War I was over, Americans eagerly sought ways to forget the devastation the war had caused so many families. The music industry provided the catharsis people wanted, and sheet music sales remained strong. So, for the first time, did record sales. By 1921, in fact, records resulted in over $106 million in sales—not bad for something that was supposed to be a passing fad.

But just as music publishers prepared for what looked like a gold mine in phonograph records, another major change occurred. It had been quite an exciting two decades, filled with motion pictures, song slides, integrated dance bands, recorded music, and more. But now, another technological advance was about to take the United States and Canada by storm: it was called *Radio*.

2

Radio's Early Years

No history of music directing could be complete without a look at the history of radio, but much of radio's earliest achievement didn't involve music. Yes, innovators like Frank Conrad and Reginald Fessenden did transmit musical selections (Conrad even played some phonograph records), but the original purpose of radio experiments was to prove that voice, not just Morse code, could be transmitted with Marconi's exciting invention, the wireless. The first target audience was ships at sea, and Reginald Fessenden amazed them when he was able, in 1906, to broadcast both voice and music. It wasn't until 1919 that anything resembling radio as we know it today began. XWA (later CFCF) in Montreal in 1919, followed soon after by KDKA in Pittsburgh in 1920, were the first such pioneers; KDKA is acknowledged as the first U.S. station with regularly scheduled programming (although, like most early stations, it was only on for a few hours each evening). The first big events that radio offered were not musical: KDKA broadcast presidential election returns in 1920. CKAC in Montreal became known in the early 1920s for its live broadcasts of church services for shut-ins, something KDKA also did. Sports programming was also popular: championship boxing matches and baseball games were on the air as early as 1921. And since the critics wanted radio to be educational, many early stations offered numerous talks by professors or experts on a variety of uplifting topics. WGN in Chicago, owned by a newspaper, offered news broadcasts as early as 1922 as well as stock reports. In the farm belt, stations like WHO in Des Moines and KMA in Shenandoah, Iowa, provided programs of interest to farmers. As for music, while most stations had some, it was inconsistently done. Some stations let almost any amateur musician appear. Others had their own professional orchestras. At a time when spoken-word programs abounded, radio was just learning how to bring music to the ever-growing number of listeners. Early stations not only had limited hours to be on the air, but most also had low power; and while radio was experiencing dramatic growth in the early 1920s, many people still didn't have their own radio receiver. (Also, early receivers, like early broadcasts, were rather primitive in their technical quality, but radio was such an exciting new medium that most people didn't object.) Then, there was the problem inherent in any new medium: there weren't any rules about how to do it right, so much experimenting occurred. The critics said radio should teach the masses about "good music," so stations like WWJ broadcast entire live performances of symphony orchestras; as early as February of 1922, the station was airing the Detroit Symphony. Across the country in Stockton, California, station KWG offered live performances of opera singers as early as 1921.

Famous sopranos sang at a number of the early stations, in fact, despite how impos-
ing the first studios looked, with their tangled maze of wires and dials and no audience except an engineer. (For this reason, studio audiences were created, because
performers felt so uncomfortable standing in front of a huge microphone in a virtually silent room.) In addition to classical vocalists, violin soloists and pianists were
also staples at many of the first stations. (In the South, despite critical protestations,
many radio stations avoided classical music and instead offered local Country and
Western musicians.) Just as respectable clubs during the dance crazes of 1912–14
were expected to have a good dance band, it wasn't long before the custom of allowing any willing singer to perform gave way to the expectation that a good station
would have its own live orchestra. Many stations did (in Hartford, WTIC's orchestra
became very famous), but in some of the smaller cities, it was often difficult to find
enough talent to make up a good orchestra. In the farm belt, stations often relied on
local fiddlers and bluegrass groups. Elsewhere, stations like WOWO in Fort Wayne
and WBT in Charlotte became known for their ability to give the best country musicians much-needed exposure, which could even result in stardom. Although some
stations became famous for their radio dramas and others for their sports broadcasts,
gradually it was music that provided the majority of the entertainment on radio. And
once the novelty wore off, most stations abandoned attempts to play what was educational and gave the audience what was popular. America had seen a ragtime craze
and a dance craze. Now, in the 1920s, there was a radio craze, as over 700 stations
were competing for listeners. Needless to say, Tin Pan Alley saw yet another great
opportunity for selling sheet music.

But what about records, you may ask? If not every station had a live orchestra,
and if as early as 1920, Frank Conrad of KDKA had played records and allowed
listeners to write in their requests, why weren't records the first choice of broadcasters? There were several factors to consider. As you know, phonograph records were
being made in the 1890s, and some highly respected classical and opera performers
made use of this new method of letting their music be heard. Records had the benefit
of allowing listeners to enjoy a song over and over in the privacy of their own home,
rather than having to go to a theater or a vaudeville show. Phonograph records became more popular during the dance craze, as people wanted to purchase the songs
in addition to the sheet music so they could master the new dance steps. Where at
first it was mainly "good music" that had been recorded, by 1914, it was a common
occurrence to hear the popular songs of the day. The bad news is that phonograph
records still suffered from rather primitive technology. The early record players had
a big tin horn that collected the sound, a metal needle, and a rotating wax cylinder
(early records were not the flat discs to which we have become accustomed). In
addition to sounding rather tinny and distorted to our ears, early records had another
problem: in most cases, they couldn't accommodate a song that was longer than four
minutes. For a popular song that was no problem, but for classical pieces it definitely
was. In order to hear a long selection, a listener would have to get up and change the
disc several times, thus breaking the mood. This gave live radio orchestras a great
advantage, one that they held during the next music craze of the 1920s, the rise of
jazz. But before we turn to the popularity of jazz, more needs to be said about
records. Many early stations did try to play them, but since this at first required putting a microphone up to the record player (which didn't have great sound quality to

begin with), you can see why records didn't immediately cause a sensation. Radio listeners were becoming more sophisticated as more competition for their loyalty came along. The perception continued to exist that live music was better and had more class than playing a phonograph record. Economically speaking, music on the radio was free once you bought a receiver, while records had to be bought continually. New and improved technology, plus the impact of the jukebox, rescued phonograph records as we will see later. Meanwhile radio stations were cautious, as they discovered the tastes of their audience. The inventor of the phonograph, Thomas Edison, provided one final reason why records didn't become an overnight sensation: Edison stated emphatically that he hated the way recorded music sounded on radio. In fact, he predicted that radio would only be useful for the spoken word (news, educational talks), while people would soon grow tired of this radio fad and return to their phonograph when they wanted to have music in their home.

By the mid 1920s, radio had become widely accepted as the best way for the average person to hear the newest songs. As with sheet music, a hit was defined by how much demand there was for it. The song pluggers had long since found ways to get famous singers to perform specific selections during vaudeville shows. Now that radio had proved it was not going to go away, the pluggers began making use of the new medium, just as they had with vaudeville. They would offer money to well-known singers to perform a given song on a radio show; they would also offer money if that artist would make a phonograph record of the song. They appealed to the artist's ego with large pictures of the artist on the sheet music. In the 1920s, paying money to a famous singer was not yet seen as bribery, nor was it illegal. It was regarded as part of doing business, much like lobbying. With the advent of the radio networks in the late 1920s, pluggers saw an even bigger chance to get their songs heard: they began making friends with band leaders. This too was simply looked upon as a necessary business expense. In an excellent history of what we today call *payola*, Professor R.H. Coase of the University of Chicago Law School noted, "The only means of directly influencing the content of music programs was for the publisher or song writer to pay dance band leaders to play selected items. Those who were unable to make such payments were simply left out."[1] Band leaders were also paid to plug a song by stepping up to the microphone and saying something good about it. As early as 1916, he continues, there were some efforts to end song payments. A group called the Music Publishers' Protective Association (MPPA) was formed, with its stated purpose to "promote and foster clean and free competition among music publishers by eradicating the evil custom of paying tribute or gratuities to singers or musicians."[2] It was a noble concept, but the MPPA was unable to enforce its own rules, and song payments simply became less blatant. They did, however, continue, and the band leaders continued to profit, as they told millions of network radio listeners about a new song they were really excited about.

The 1920s not only saw the massive growth of radio; they also saw more dance crazes and the impact of yet another black musical genre, jazz. Ragtime had burnt itself out. America was ready for the next thing, and jazz was definitely it. Pure jazz, played by the great black musicians of New Orleans, Chicago, and New York developed a devoted cult following among whites. Jazz, also known as *swing*, was another up-tempo musical form, which was known for the way its players improvised while performing it. That improvisational, creative style made it very exciting to watch.

But once again, what made jazz into a mass-appeal music involved a white group. Just as Ben Harney had made ragtime popular with whites, so the Original Dixieland Jazz Band (ODJB) brought jazz into the middle-class mainstream. ODJB was comprised of five white men from New Orleans who loved and respected Black music. When they brought their talents to the clubs of New York, they proved immensely popular. Soon jazz bands were appearing virtually everywhere. And yes, you could dance to jazz. In fact, this new craze led to several new dances, one of which was quite controversial—it was called the shimmy. Several people claim to have first performed this dance, but the best known was probably Gilda Gray, already a popular singer and dancer when she joined ODJB as their lead vocalist. She began doing the shimmy on stage with the band in 1920, and caused an immediate stir because the dance involved body movements that were much more sexual than any previous dances. Actually, versions of this dance had been around for years, but once a popular celebrity performed it, that made it all right for the average person to do it too. While conservative critics again lamented the moral breakdown in society and expressed horror that women were shaking and shimmying so much on the dance floor, the dance became a hit, and Tin Pan Alley was able to provide a number of appropriate songs for the occasion, as they always had with other dance crazes. But this time something new was available: radio airplay. Thanks to radio, for the first time, hit songs weren't available only to the club-going crowd. A much wider audience could hear and enjoy them (and then, the publishers hoped, buy the sheet music). Rather than seeing radio as competition, music publishers saw it as one more tool to make their songs more popular. They weren't quite sure what impact radio airplay would have, but they were certainly willing to find out.

As music publishers and song pluggers watched radio become a major force, other ways of promoting songs were also becoming factors. Movies were still silent—that is, spoken dialogue was not yet possible, but background music was and continued to be. Music publishers had wasted no time making friends with moviemakers and studio executives so that the right theme song would be used as background. Since music was an established part of moviegoing (song slides were still being used at theaters), it was more good news when cartoons became popular. What did cartoons have to do with promoting songs? Interestingly, a respected cartoonist named Max Fleischer (who gave us such unforgettable characters as Popeye and Betty Boop) teamed with his brother Dave to create cartoons that could be used with music. These were much more fun to watch than song slides, since cartoons had movement, while song slides showed singers posing. By 1924, the so-called *bouncing ball* series was born: this clever idea enabled theatergoers to learn the words to a new song as they sang along, following an animated dot which moved in syncopated time on top of each word displayed on the screen. As the song played in the background and the cartoon characters acted it out, the audience was given a much more memorable way of becoming familiar with the song. A number of hits (and a few non-hits) were introduced via cartoons.

While more dance crazes occurred, among them the Charleston, there was a growing backlash against so-called immoral dances. And even people who didn't find the latest dances particularly lewd wanted a change from all that frantic movement. This led to a rise in popularity of some conservative dance bands that played music couples could enjoy in a dignified manner. The critics were busily trying to have jazz banned from radio, meanwhile, and station owners were struggling with trying to find out exactly what the audience wanted. Early program directors may have lacked research, but their instincts told them the average person didn't want to be educated by radio. People wanted entertainment. And for most people, that didn't mean classical music or professors lecturing. Fortunately, the music of the dance bands solved the problem. The best known of these bands was that of Paul Whiteman. He and his band played a melodic and mass appeal music that was influenced by jazz and yet was rather pretty. Whiteman, ironically, became known as the King of Jazz, even though he personally disliked pure jazz and the music his band played bore little resemblance to that music. Whiteman's band made many records, which sold well, and they also performed in vaudeville theaters and at the finest dancing establishments. Radio stations began playing some of these songs, and they were well received. Paul Whiteman also made an impact in several other ways: his band was the place a number of important musicians got their first exposure, and he himself became a VIP to the song-plugging community. It became obvious that having Whiteman's band perform a song could turn it into a major hit.

As radio stations tried hard to give the public what it wanted, they discovered that radio could go where the audience was. Like record promotion (and song plugging was still more important than promoting records, since every artist needed songs but not every artist made records yet), station promotion was still developing. KDKA in Pittsburgh was probably the first U.S. station to do a remote broadcast. It wasn't long before stations were setting up equipment in hotel ballrooms so they could broadcast the music of some well-known dance band while giving the station some much-needed visibility. For reasons of visibility, in fact, several major radio stations (including KDKA and WCCO in Minneapolis) had their studios in a hotel (a much better location than the rooftop studios KDKA first had in its earliest days).

While the audiences at home enjoyed the music of the dance bands, and while the musicians were pleased about this new way of exposing their talents to people both in a hall and in homes all over the area, there were some problems. For one, not every band was famous: some weren't even very good. There was also human nature: even then, when people liked a song they wanted a repeat performance. With live performances there was no choice (and few fans realized that the song pluggers had probably influenced what songs the band would perform that night): what the band played was what you got to hear. This fact was not lost on radio's first program directors. When a song seemed to get good response at the dance hall, program directors would seek out the recorded version, if there was one. The idea of taking requests was thus not a new one: as early as 1922, for example, Charlotte (North Carolina) newspapers talking about the first broadcasts of WBT mentioned that the station played certain phonograph records by request. In late 1921, we are also told, phonograph records served another function that those of us in radio know well: they filled for time. After a live concert by a certain famous soprano, station KWG in Stockton (California) followed immediately with all of her records. Despite Mr. Edison's concerns, there were quite a few early stations that made some use of records. But controversies soon arose. Where records allowed people to have some control over what was heard in the home (if parents didn't want their children to do the shimmy, for example, all they had to do was hide the shimmy records), radio had elements of the unknown. Perhaps the singer would do a performance of a classical aria; but then, perhaps the singer would perform a vaudeville number that wasn't fit for tender young ears. Despite the so-called *Roaring Twenties* and their fabled permissiveness, there were still many conservative citizens (remember Prohibition?). These people encouraged censorship of songs they considered suggestive, and entire lines of popular songs had to be changed to meet their requirements. Radio stations complied, partially because many owners wanted to position radio as a safe, family-oriented medium and they thus wanted to avoid all controversy. The other reason they didn't protest was the advertisers: once sponsorship of programs became commonly accepted, stations were especially cautious about airing anything that a sponsor might dislike. So-called *hot jazz* (the traditional black music with all its energy and improvisation) was considered too dangerous to play on radio as a result. Music on radio quickly leaned toward what was cynically referred to as the *potted-palm* variety, named after the plants that hotels and some radio studios placed in strategic locations to hide the huge microphones that often intimidated vocalists. Potted-palm music was melodic, bland, and without a trace of the risqué. Radio stations split into two camps—those who were still trying to program "good music" (especially classical and opera), many of which had their own regular performers (local symphony musicians) as well as a live orchestra; and those who had decided to give the people what they wanted (WSB in Atlanta, for example, which played country music from the day it went on the air in 1922), even if that included jazz.

In the first years of radio, the people we now call *program directors* (PDs) were seldom hired for their musical knowledge. Some were engineers; others were business or professional people. A few were educators, and there were some with backgrounds in public relations. Some of the owners also wore many hats, including that of PD. As a result of the divergence in their experience, and the lack of an official job description, some of the early PDs created the position as they went along, and the station's programming followed along the lines of their own expertise. Thus, Minneapolis's first radio station, WLAG, went on the air in 1922 with Eleanor Poehler as its managing director. Her background was as a voice teacher and soprano at the MacPhail School of Music. The station had a studio orchestra, but it did not own any records: instead, it borrowed them from the department stores which sponsored broadcasts. Mrs. Poehler was adamant about what kind of music WLAG played: nothing but classical and conservatory music. She refused to play country music, calling it a curse, and she regarded all forms of popular music with disdain. In fact, in the book *Sixty Years Strong* by Larry Haeg, Jr. (a fascinating history of Minneapolis's second and best-known station, WCCO), the official voice of the MacPhail School of Music, William MacPhail, is quoted as saying this about popular music: "[It is] atrociously suggestive trash which jeopardizes the moral fibre of every American home." [3] To further demonstrate that WLAG's mission was to uplift the audience, Mrs. Poehler insisted on a full *15 seconds* of silence between each song and the announcer, evidently to give the audience time to fully appreciate the song before the commonplace announcer had to intrude. (WLAG went off the air in 1924, almost bankrupt.) In Cedar Rapids, meanwhile, WJAM (later WMT) went on the air from a converted garage in the summer of 1922, with few pretensions: the first song the station ever played was a popular but forgettable ditty called "Don't Bring Me Posies When It's Shoes-ies That I Need." WJAM was one of the first farm-belt stations to have a jazz show, and its friendly, folksy style of broadcasting quickly made it the most popular station in town. A similar phenomenon occurred at KMA in Shenandoah, another of Iowa's many early stations. KMA too programmed a wide variety of music—all live, most of it either popular or country. Because it was in a small town, KMA was at first restricted to broadcasting for only one hour at noon, one hour each evening, and two hours on Tuesday and Thursday nights. (Bear in mind that until 1927, radio stations had few rules about where or when they could broadcast. Some stations had to share the same frequency, with one going off the air so that another could have its turn. This led to chaos, as bigger stations boosted their power and drowned out smaller ones on a regular basis. Also, not all owners or managers were good about sharing: Eleanor Poehler tried to prevent a new competitor in Minneapolis from buying equipment necessary to go on the air, while in Canada, it was reported that two Toronto station owners got into a fistfight when one felt the other had refused to relinquish the airwaves in a timely fashion.) During KMA's first week of programs in 1925, the small station still made a big impact, using *175* live performers, including Gertrude May (the wife of station founder Earl May, she was an accomplished singer and businesswoman in her own right), The How Do You Do Boys, Floyd and Jessie Young, the Municipal Band, and May's Mandolin Musicians, all of whom offered a wide range of selections from hymns to dance music and country fiddle tunes. Earl May's commitment was that his new station would never be monotonous, and to that end, KMA offered a great variety of programs, some musical and others educational, all aimed at the mostly farm-oriented audience it served. Earl May not only oversaw KMA's operation, but he also did some announcing and helped line up guest speakers (to give informative talks about subjects that farmers would find useful). He also broadcast farm and market reports, and helped set up news and sports reporting on the station. What he did not do was choose the music. From what we can tell about those early days, the musicians themselves came up with a musical program, although certain songs were often requested. KMA was very late in playing records; as a result, the station built up a large number of talented local groups, many of which performed for free just to get some exposure. These regulars also played around the area, and had certain songs with which the audience identified them from having attended live performances. The local musicians played mostly the popular songs of the day, as well as whatever new songs they may have encountered. But at that point, there is no evidence to suggest that Earl May or any other KMA official mandated a definite music policy: so long as the audience was happy and entertained, all was well at KMA.

But things were not well in the music industry. The sudden and unexpected radio craze had put a serious dent in phonograph record sales. Vaudeville was also suffering, as were sales of sheet music. Amid these changes, an organization called the American Society of Composers, Authors and Publishers (ASCAP) became influential. Its actual beginnings went back to 1909, the year the Copyright Act gave publishers and composers the right to collect royalties on songs that were performed in public. This was a result of the various dance halls that had sprung up all over the country, all of which were using music, but few of which were paying anything to the people who had written or published the songs. In the earlier days of American music, when travel wasn't so common and there weren't so many venues, a songwriter could simply appear at a performance and pass the hat. But that was now impossible, and something had to be done to make sure royalties were paid. ASCAP itself wasn't officially formed until 1914, but the Copyright Act of 1909 had set the appropriate precedent. ASCAP's purpose was to take it a step further and make certain that the hard-working residents of Tin Pan Alley received their fair share of the successful music business. It seemed that everywhere, music had become a part of daily life. Even restaurants played music, and ASCAP first tested its strength in 1914 by taking one New York establishment to court for not paying royalties on the music it played for its customers. The restaurant, Shanley's, and several others that ASCAP also sued, claimed it served food not music. But after a protracted court case that ultimately reached the Supreme Court, Justice Oliver Wendell Holmes ruled in 1917 in favor of ASCAP; restaurants, as well as dance clubs, could no longer perform songs without paying royalties. Since radio was still rather new in the early 1920s, it took a little while for ASCAP to formulate a strategy, but by 1922 the members of ASCAP, worried about the decline in vaudeville attendance (it was easier to stay home and hear all the famous celebrities on the radio) and the decline in sheet music sales (now radio, not the family piano, was the main source of entertainment in the average middle-class home), decided that radio had gotten a free ride long enough. Where ASCAP had at first regarded radio as a harmless fad that would soon fade away, and offered little protest about radio plugging songs for a while at no cost, suddenly it became obvious that radio wasn't going away and pianos weren't about to experience a resurgence. So, ASCAP took a few carefully selected stations to court. Many broadcasters were puzzled by ASCAP's new stance: as they saw it, they couldn't afford to pay royalties (running a station was extremely expensive); plus, they continued, rather than hurting sheet music or phonograph records, radio airplay exposed new songs to millions of people and actually provided a major benefit. But ASCAP disagreed, and soon, so did the courts. Upset by the outcome of the case, a group of broadcasters met in Chicago in 1923, determined to establish their own organization to fight ASCAP's power. This group was at first very small and not especially effective against ASCAP, but the National Association of Broadcasters (NAB) would continue to grow, as radio did, and they would eventually confront ASCAP again, as we shall see.

   With broadcasters now having to pay ASCAP, some stations stopped using ASCAP-licensed songs. To further complicate matters, ASCAP became more convinced that radio airplay would be detrimental to record sales: Why buy a record (thereby providing royalties for some ASCAP member) when a person could hear it on radio for nothing? ASCAP wanted records to be designated for home use only, with radio stations using only live performances (which kept many musicians working). Meanwhile, ASCAP had collected over $800,000 from radio for music performance fees in the year 1930 alone.

   The late 1920s made a further impact on music, as well as on radio as a medium. The year 1927 stands out for several reasons. For one, that year, the Federal Radio Commission (FRC) was founded, to establish some order in the chaotic environment created by too many stations operating with too few rules. The FRC had its failings, but it did allocate definite frequencies and definite power outputs for stations, so they could no longer move around the AM dial as they pleased or drown each other out (which was excellent news for Canada—some of the U.S. stations that had unscrupulously raised power regularly caused major interference for unsuspecting Canadian stations). Also, the FRC stated plainly that from now on, while it was fine for stations to make a profit, they could not ignore the needs of their community nor avoid serving the public. Another important event in 1927 was the development of the talking picture. The first motion picture to utilize this new technology was Al Jolson's *The Jazz Singer*, which, strictly speaking, wasn't a talking picture—it was a singing picture. But it was the first time that sound had been synchronized with the actor moving his lips, and it paved the way for the use of actual spoken dialogue. Jolson was to the 1920s what Frank Sinatra was to the 1940s: in those pre–rock and roll years, certain singers attained almost mythical stature. Like the rock stars of today (only, in most cases, not so temporary), these idols could make a song a hit just by singing it. Al Jolson, needless to say, was eagerly sought after by song pluggers, all of whom were positive they had his next big hit; Jolson also benefited from the song pluggers' largesse, because he was sometimes given songwriting royalties even though he never wrote a song. But this was what the pluggers felt they had to do to make sure Jolson would perform their songs. And Jolson wasn't the only idol who had this expectation. (Remember that in those days the system of rewarding the big singers and band leaders with gifts or money was *not* illegal.)

The same year that *The Jazz Singer* ended the era of silent movies, 1927, was also a big year for yet another invention that would be of immense help to the music industry. The jukebox (as it would later be called) wasn't new; in fact, it had been around in various incarnations since the early 1900s, when it was known as the *automatic phonograph*. Like early recorded music, the first jukeboxes lacked good sound quality, but they were still quite popular in saloons and taverns. In 1927, a major advance in technology occurred: electrical amplification. What this meant was that now the machine could play loudly and clearly enough to entertain an entire room, and all you needed was a nickel. Suddenly, the automatic phonograph (the name *jukebox* wasn't widely used until the 1930s, and there is considerable debate as to the word's origin) was in direct competition with orchestras and dance bands. This made dance-hall owners happy because while it was expensive to hire a band, now it was possible to keep large numbers of customers satisfied just by having a jukebox and the records the clientele liked. Jukeboxes became a good reason why people went to certain clubs. The owners of these clubs fulfilled a function similar to music directing or club disc jockeying: they picked the songs for people to dance to. It was an important job. With so many places buying jukeboxes, what made a club unique was the selection of music. Some clubs distinguished themselves by offering music that radio would not yet play—blues, for example. Southern owners made sure country fiddle tunes were available. There were even some off-color (or more accurately, obscene) songs aimed specifically at the male audience that frequented certain saloons, and these too received jukebox play. In some ways, the jukeboxes became the medium of choice for playing alternative music as well as for enabling people to hear their favorite songs over and over. While this just seemed like good business sense on the part of club owners in the 1930s, it would lead to the development of Top-40 radio in the 1950s, as we shall soon see. Once again, inventions and business decisions made many years earlier would lead to trends that still influence our lives in the 1990s.

And what was radio doing during this innovative time? It was still trying to define its role in society, as critics condemned it and accused it of playing the wrong music or being a bad influence on the young. Radio's PDs were eager to prove that their stations could make a positive impact on their community. The emergence of the networks brought a better quality of entertainment, including many famous performers, and helped local stations sound as good as those in big cities. Thanks to NBC and CBS, listeners were offered soap operas, radio dramas, and even comedy, as well as the best-known dance bands. (By the way, if you think I forgot a network, ABC didn't come along until later. Mutual arrived first, bringing with it some excellent programs aimed at kids, but beloved by adults too, such as "The Lone Ranger" and "The Green Hornet.")

Radio was a part of virtually everyone's life. Families gathered around their radio (one room in the home was even called the *radio room*) to hear their favorite shows. But what did the listeners want? Once the novelty of radio's early days wore off, it became important to please the audience or they might listen to some other station. As early as 1923, Chicago radio stations such as KYW were taking surveys to find out the preferences of their audience. The results were rather interesting, and still applicable today: despite the hopes of professors and critics, people overwhelmingly said they wanted music, not educational talks.

Listeners did want to be informed, however, and they were fascinated by how quickly radio could report an event or a news story. You could get the baseball scores as they happened, which was impossible with the newspaper. Information and news programs were added slowly: in the late 1920s, most stations didn't even do news on a regular basis. They saw their niche as an entertainment medium, a respite from the scandal-sheet attitude of the tabloid newspapers (yes, there were tabloids even back then), something the entire family could use and enjoy. But early programming on radio was not very scientific. PDs tried something, and if listeners seemed to like it, it stayed; otherwise, it was removed. Thus we find that in Chicago in the late 1920s, programming schedules showed stations that ran synagogue services, live broadcasts of the County Fair, political speeches, on-air college courses in sociology, baseball, and broadcasts of the symphony orchestra. Several Canadian stations were affiliated with a U.S. network to take advantage of the famous performers that CBS and NBC offered. Network radio was booming: NBC and CBS had affiliates from coast to coast by the late 1920s, in cities of all sizes. Perhaps their most unusual affiliate was one of the Canadian stations, trend-setting CKAC in Montreal, a station that broadcast only in French. When the station aired network shows, announcers would translate any comments or dialogue into French. But fortunately, music is universal, and the famous stars were just as well known in Canada as anywhere else. CKAC also used phonograph records, in addition to its own local bands, theater groups, hotel orchestras, and sports commentators; most of CKAC's record library came from France, which had had a thriving recording industry since the turn of the century. CKAC's experiences, both good and bad, with affiliating with a U.S. network (they chose CBS) led them to create a network for French Canadian stations, and pioneer news broadcasting as well. (Canada wouldn't get its first national network, the Canadian Broadcasting Corporation, or CBC, until 1936, which also explains why some Canadian stations felt a U.S. network was better than none at all.)

As radio became more and more popular, the record companies feared they were on the verge of becoming obsolete. Actually, the opposite occurred. After several lean years, during which the novelty of the new medium made people listen to anything radio offered, records made a comeback, since people still wanted to have access to their favorite songs. It took the record companies a while, however, before they saw radio as their ally, not their adversary. Until 1924, major record labels, still unable to see that airplay could lead to sales, went so far as to prevent radio from using records. Companies like Victor Talking Machine forbade their artists to perform on radio; they believed free exposure would diminish the public's desire to buy records. But popular songs were not a one-time pleasure for the average person. Even in the 1920s, a hit was a hit, and people didn't mind hearing the song again (witness the impact the jukebox made). With no radio play, the Victor Talking Machine company watched record sales decline dramatically. Finally, in 1924, they faced reality, noting that if radio advertising could sell all sorts of goods and services successfully, why couldn't it be used to sell records?

By January of 1925, the company's two biggest stars, opera singer Lucrezia Bori and Irish tenor John McCormack, made their debuts in special live performances over New York's WEAF and a network of other stations that joined for this historic broadcast. The concert was built up beforehand with newspaper and radio ads that invited people to purchase the two singers' recordings. If Victor needed any proof that radio exposure was a plus not a minus, the week following that concert told the story best: over 200,000 copies of their records were sold. In case the sheet music publishers felt left out, they needn't have worried—one new song John McCormack introduced during the WEAF performance ("All Alone," written by Irving Berlin) went on to sell 100,000 copies in an amazingly short time. Needless to say, Victor was delighted, so much so that the company allowed more of its artists to perform, with the same results: more records were sold, and the sheet music to certain songs also became big sellers. Soon, several more record companies had abandoned their unofficial boycott of radio, determined that if they couldn't beat them, they definitely could join them. It was a good move for all concerned, as radio received an infusion of major talent, performers with wide-ranging repertoires who could offer beautiful operatic selections yet still have mass appeal and do some popular songs. As with records and jukeboxes, radio too had vastly improved technology, which made these concerts even more enjoyable to the home listener. Such improvements came at a good time: with motion pictures now offering sound, radio's clear reception and its excellent assortment of name talent kept the medium competitive.

Radio in the late 1920s began to use its influence to help expose the stars of tomorrow, with network shows like NBC's "National Radio Auditions" and "The Palmolive Hour;" the latter sponsored by a soap company, was one of the first shows to feature the week's biggest hits, performed by a group of studio musicians, many of whom went on to become successful on their own. "The Palmolive Hour" became so popular that people would line up in front of NBC's New York studio in hopes of obtaining tickets to be part of the studio audience. The show quickly became an excellent vehicle for introducing new songs, much as vaudeville had once been, and quite a few of the songs performed on the show did become hits. All this was no accident, as is evident from the discussion about song pluggers in Chapter 1. The question of whether radio airplay helped or hurt records and sheet music had been answered.

Musical comedies were also popular in the late 1920s; during the 1927-1928 season alone, 53 were performed on Broadway, providing more opportunities for the great composers of the day to introduce their new songs. These songs would also be heard on radio and purchased as records and sheet music. The entertainment industry was booming, with Tin Pan Alley enjoying enormous success and huge profits. Any performer who made regular appearances on radio, any band leader with a weekly show could be certain the song pluggers would be there to woo them. As Al Jolson had discovered, the more popular a performer was, the more demand there was for his or her sheet music and records. And the more likelihood there was that an enterprising promoter would find a way to persuade those big stars to perform (and by now, to record) certain new songs. Eddie Cantor became one of radio's most sought-after performers during the 1920s, continuing his successful career well into radio's so-called *Golden Age*, the 1930s through the mid-1940s, an era dominated by famous radio comedians, dramatic actors and actresses, and big bands with their superstar vocalists. Eddie Cantor became yet another performer whose popularity was so great that having him sing a certain song virtually assured that song's success; this was also true of crooner Rudy Vallee. Exposure on the networks made these and other vocalists into national heroes: no longer did singers have to build their careers by singing in clubs in hundreds of cities. By becoming regulars on the networks they enhanced their popularity greatly, and made themselves more important in the eyes of the song pluggers. It was a time when popular vocalists, as opposed to opera singers, really began to emerge. Among the most successful in the 1920s were Sophie Tucker (who called herself the Last of the Red Hot Mamas, because of her intense vocal style and energetic stage presence) and Louis Armstrong (who would still be making hit records 40 years later).

The 1930s were the years of the Great Depression, but they were boom years for radio, movies, and the music industry. Since most people could no longer afford to attend the theater, they turned to radio more than ever for their entertainment. And since times were so hard, when they could afford to go out they wanted to forget their troubles and escape into a world where people were happy and love conquered all. Movie musicals (some with elaborate dance routines) became especially popular during the Depression, and songs from these movies went on to become hits on radio.

Meanwhile, there were still more changes in store for the music industry. Perhaps the most important for us today involved a group of people we take for granted now, but back then, they were not the celebrities they are now. The Depression years gradually brought to the forefront the use of records over live music, and that led to a new radio job: a *disc jockey*.

Notes

1. Coase, R.H. "Payola in Radio and Television Broadcasting." *Journal of Law and Economics,* University of Chicago Law School. Volume 22, #2, 1979, pp. 269328.
2. *Ibid.*
3. Haeg, Larry, Jr. *Sixty Years Strong.* Minneapolis: WCCO Radio, 1984.

3

▼ The Announcers
▼
▼
▼
▼

As we have seen thus far, picking the music for radio was a rather undefined, hit-or-miss proposition in that industry's first decade. In fact, song pluggers and jukebox owners probably had more to say about what songs would be heard than any radio program director. PDs scheduled guests, but they didn't seem to have any rules about what music those guests would perform. Obviously, as time went on, common sense prevailed. If an artist or band got excellent response with a certain song during live performances, PDs would be sure to suggest that the song be performed on radio shows. As more records were recorded, it became easier to follow up a live concert with a few of that artist's hits. But still, radio stations of the 1930s hadn't yet switched over to all records, and announcers were still doing mainly announcing, without the personality elements we associate with radio today. There were still no official rules (which today are known as *formatics*) about where to give the weather or tell the time, or even when to say the station's call letters. Stations didn't have the cute names they would during the Top-40 era in the 1950s and 60s: there was no "Q103" or "Z94," no "The Fox" or "The Rock and Roll Animal." But even in the 30s, there were some innovators who were setting the stage for the style of radio we today know so well.

Vocalists still dominated the networks: Kate Smith had a number of pop hits. Soprano Jessica Dragonette made light opera understandable for the average listener, and was so well received that she was voted "The Queen of Radio" in one national magazine's fan poll. And a new form of dance music called *Swing* was taking over. Swing was up-tempo and energetic, but it wasn't as frenetic as some of the other dance crazes had been. It was performed by dance bands that were much larger than earlier incarnations: for obvious reasons, these came to be known as *Big Bands*. Their leaders became stars too, and had legions of adoring young fans. Among the most popular of the Big Band leaders were Artie Shaw, Benny Goodman, and Glenn Miller. This was an especially interesting trend, because prior to this point, only the popular singers were idolized; now, every young person seemed to have a favorite band and a favorite band leader. This also introduced the power of young people as a force in creating hits. Radio programming had been directed at adults most of the time. Swing, however, was popular with a younger audience, who went to see the performers and requested their records faithfully: several band leaders found they now had their own official fan clubs. While this was occurring, it is doubtful radio's PDs saw it as a trend, but it was to be an important event for later radio programming; for the first time, a musical fad had been started and maintained entirely by young people. The devotion young adults showed to swing (they even developed a language called *jive talk*, and they also had their own mode of dress, much as rock and rollers would during the 50s) proved that the music industry had an entirely new, and up until now, underserved audience.

As for radio, the days of experimentation with all opera or all symphony orchestras (except on a few educational and college stations) had ended, and while the concept of *format* was undefined, most stations had settled into a combination of popular music (big band and vocalists in some cities, country music in others), sports, public service, a little news, and of course, commercials. AM radio ruled: there had been a few engineers who were aware of the possibilities of something called FM, but that wasn't a major priority in the 1930s. There were now ratings available, so that the networks had some idea what the most popular shows were. Locally, stations had active listeners who were quick to praise or complain.

It is those vocal listeners to whom we owe the increased popularity of announcers. In radio's first few years, owners didn't even allow announcers to give their names: they were only identified by their initials. If you are a trivia fan, you'll be pleased to know that the first announcer was probably Tommy Cowan of Station WJZ in New York, in 1921; but his listeners knew him as ACN (Announcer *C*owan *N*ew York). Other announcers were given similar but slightly different sets of initials: theater critic and later Program Director Bertha Brainard was known as ABN, for example. The idea behind this was to keep the announcers from becoming too popular and asking the owners for more money. Unfortunately for the owners, it didn't work; even though people didn't know their names, their voices earned them loyal fans, who wrote to the stations and demanded to know who these announcers were. By 1924, announcers were using their names on a regular basis.

Early announcers were very different from what we are accustomed to now. For one thing, their job was to announce, much like a master or mistress of ceremonies. What they said was totally scripted, and was expected to be read with flawless, almost professorial diction. In fact, one of New York's first announcers, Norman Brokenshire, nearly got himself fired by daring to depart from a prepared script and giving a couple of friendly ad-libs. Early announcers were supposed to sound serious; telling jokes was for comedians only. Further, announcers were expected to wear proper dress to the studio—tuxedo for males, evening gown for females. This was somewhat ironic, given that there were not usually any studio audiences to see what they wore, but the dress code reflected the more formal attitude of society. (Imagine a formally dressed announcer climbing a ladder up to the rooftop studio where he or she was to broadcast. The idea of plush, comfortable studios that were easy to reach wasn't implemented during radio's first 3 years.)

The first announcers, in addition to working on rooftops and in such unglamorous places as garages and even tents (KDKA in Pittsburgh moved from a rooftop location to a tent before finally settling in at a local hotel), had to do a little of everything. They were combination program directors, publicists, news gatherers, and copywriters. They also booked their station's guests (and filled for time if a guest didn't show up). Some played phonograph records; others played a musical instrument. None got rich: the typical pay for an announcer in the early days of radio was between $45 and $65 a week.

Fortunately for announcers, the job quickly acquired some fringe benefits. Then as now, it was an exciting opportunity to meet famous people. In the pre-network days, celebrities who were in a particular city to do a concert would also perform on the local station, and the announcers at that station would do the introductions. Then, there were other advantages: radio historian Eric Barnouw explains in his book, *A Tower in Babel*, that radio announcers of the mid-1920s began receiving a lot more than just fan letters.

[Popular announcers] and management struggled over personal appearances as well. The rising stars were deluged with invitations. Some stations permitted announcers to appear as station representatives, but not to accept remuneration. Instead, they were plied with gifts. [One announcer received] monogrammed cigarette cases, belt buckles, and a pigskin wallet with gold corners, as well as a plaque that held a twenty dollar gold piece. . . . Everywhere, radio personalities were treated like war heroes. [Some] received keys to the city, were met with bands, and were driven through the streets in automobiles.

There were a few unique announcers, Norman Brokenshire among them, who were constantly testing the boundaries in the new medium to see what the listeners would and would not like. Many radio historians feel that Brokenshire was the fore-runner of what we call today the *air personality*, because he just couldn't stay with a dry, boring script. New York audiences found his sense of humor refreshing, and they didn't seem to mind that he didn't have an overly serious announcing style.

Another innovator was a Chicago announcer with the unusual name of Hallow-een Martin. In the late 1920s, she was one of the first to do the prototype of today's morning show. Keep in mind that, unlike today when both radio and television compete for the morning audience, in radio's early days, it was believed by the owners that people wouldn't get up early to listen to a morning show. Some stations signed on the air around 10 A.M., in fact, since they felt it would be a waste of their time to broadcast any earlier than that. The key listening times were supposedly middays when women were at hoe with their children, and evenings when after a hard day at work father would sit in the radio room and enjoy his favorite shows along with his family. Of course, this wasn't really true, but it took a few years for the myths to die. Still, in the late 1920s, a majority of stations had no particular morning show, if they even signed on that early. Halloween Martin was unique: she not only did a morning show, called "The Musical Clock," but she operated the show in a way that is re-markably close to the way morning shows are done today. She gave the time, read the weather, played up-tempo music, and even took requests. Her show was well received, considering how far ahead of its time it was.

The announcers who did play records, Ms. Martin included, seemed to have no particular rules about picking them. They did use requests as a guide, as well as availability of product (not every famous star made records, and even then, some records were more popular than others). While common sense would indicate that famous announcers met and were friendly with the song pluggers, there is little evi-dence that these pluggers concentrated much effort on announcers yet. Not all an-nouncers played records, for one thing, and for another, songs were still more important for purposes of promotion. Getting the right song to the right singer or band leader occupied the majority of the song plugger's time. Announcers were not yet part of the plan. However, they soon would be.

If the jukeboxes made a major impact in helping such genres as blues and jazz to attain a wider audience, local radio stations made an equally big contribution for country music. A few stations did program some jazz, but in general the networks and major urban centers played safe, mass-appeal pop music aimed at middle-class whites. WSM in Nashville (where the Grand Ole Opry began), WWVA in Wheeling, West Virginia, and WBT in Charlotte were among the most influential for launching the careers of country musicians. WBT earned such a reputation for finding good local talent that several record companies set up local offices in Charlotte in case some promising country singer seemed right for a recording contract. Even the small market country stations (KMA in Shenandoah, Iowa, is one good example) were very useful in exposing talented local artists. Despite the national trend toward crooners and big bands, these stations programmed what they felt their own local audience wanted.

Black music, however, was another matter. Despite a number of talented blues and jazz musicians, there was no station that concentrated on black music, and there wouldn't be until as late as the 1940s. Thus, the play provided by jukeboxes was the only opportunity for these gifted musicians to be heard, other than at live club performances. According to statistics from the early 1930s, blacks didn't fare much better in being given radio jobs: one survey could find only two black announcers in all of radio. The best-known and most influential black announcer of the 1930s was Jack Cooper, a Chicago radio pioneer who began his career as a newscaster and journalist. But music was his first love, and he finally convinced one Chicago station to air a variety show called "The All-Colored Hour." He had to get his own sponsors, which he did successfully, even in those difficult times. He next went on to play records and do a program called "The Rug-Cutter's Special" (*to cut a rug* was a slang expression for dancing), a show which soon became popular. Jack Cooper became known for his local talent shows as well as for community service in an era when blacks were still not usually hired by whites except in stereotypic roles (in movies, for example, blacks were portrayed as maids or servants). Cooper never thought of himself as a disc jockey; he felt he was a radio entrepreneur. What he also proved to be was a role model for many Chicago-area blacks who decided to enter the music industry as a result of working with him.

At the places which had jukeboxes, hearing the same song over and over wasn't a negative. In fact, how much a song was played indicated that it had hit potential. Since the average jukebox only held 24 records, this provided us with the first *playlist*. It also provided us with considerable numbers of people who had favorite records and wanted radio to play them. No longer were radio listeners content to wait for a song, nor did they only want to hear the live version. Records had made a comeback, more artists were recording, and more people had requests to make. It was time for radio to address this, as it had addressed other societal changes such as the Depression or the various dance crazes.

Chances are, the first disc jockey to play only records on a full-time basis was Al Jarvis, sometime in 1932. Although the perception that live music was somehow better still lingered on in the 1930s, Al Jarvis saw the popularity of records and decided to take a chance. Working at KFWB in Los Angeles, Jarvis began a show he

AMOA Top-40 Jukebox Singles of All Time*

Song	Artist	Year
1. Hound Dog/Don't Be Cruel	Elvis Presley	1956
2. Crazy	Patsy Cline	1961
3. Rock Around the Clock	Bill Haley & the Comets	1955
4. The Dock of the Bay	Otis Redding	1968
5. I Heard It Through the Grapevine	Marvin Gaye	1968
6. Mack the Knife	Bobby Darin	1959
7. Light My Fire	The Doors	1967
8. Blueberry Hill	Fats Domino	1956
9. Old Time Rock & Roll	Bob Seger	1979
10. My Girl	The Temptations	1965
11. Walk on the Wild Side	Lou Reed	1973
12. Honky Tonk Women	Rolling Stones	1969
13. Can't Buy Me Love	The Beatles	1964
14. New York, New York	Frank Sinatra	1980
15. Born to be Wild	Steppenwolf	1968
16. Louie, Louie	Kingsmen	1963
17. Maybellene	Chuck Berry	1955
18. Hey Jude	The Beatles	1968
19. Good Vibrations	Beach Boys	1966
20. Respect	Aretha Franklin	1967
21. Stand By Your Man	Tammy Wynette	1968
22. House of the Rising Sun	The Animals	1964
23. In the Mood	Glen Miller Orchestra	1939
24. Satisfaction	Rolling Stones	1965
25. Take Me to the River	Talking Heads	1978
26. Proud Mary	Creedence Clearwater Revival	1969
27. Bad Moon Rising	Creedence Clearwater Revival	1969
28. Jailhouse Rock	Elvis Presley	1957
29. For the Good Times	Ray Price	1970
30. Great Balls of Fire	Jerry Lee Lewis	1957
31. I Fall to Pieces	Patsy Cline	1961
32. Johnny B. Goode	Chuck Berry	1955
33. Bad to the Bone	George Thorogood	1982
34. That'll Be the Day	Buddy Holly	1957
35. The Twist	Chubby Checker	1955
36. All Shook Up	Elvis Presley	1957
37. Peggy Sue	Buddy Holly	1957
38. Heart of Gold	Neil Young	1972
39. When a Man Loves a Woman	Percy Sledge	1968
40. Star Dust	Artie Shaw	1942

*Copyright 1988. Amusement & Music Operators Association

▶ *Figure 1* AMOA Top-40 Jukebox Singles of All Time, issued as part of the centennial celebration of the jukebox, shows the influence jukeboxes have had on music for many years. (Reprinted by permission of the Amusement and Music Operators Association.)

named "The World's Largest Make-Believe Ballroom." He created for listeners a fantasy concert that featured all the major celebrities of the day, except in reality it was only their records the audience was hearing. Still, Jarvis's you-are-there approach caught on: many people weren't even aware he was doing each concert from an assortment of phonograph records. (And if you are saying to yourself that listeners must have been gullible in those days, consider this: in the late 1970s, several major-market album rock stations ran a feature known as "The Concert from Fantasy Park," wherein the live performance records of certain major rock groups were played, and the so-called event was promoted to listeners as if it were an actual concert. Although certain of the groups hadn't performed in years, listeners called their favorite station to ask how to get to Fantasy Park and how to buy tickets.)

While Al Jarvis was doing his early experiments with disc jockeying, a news reporter at KFWB was watching with great interest. His name was martin Block, and he was very impressed with Jarvis. Several years later, Block had moved from LA to New York, and was working at WNEW, when opportunity knocked. It was 1935, Block was still doing news, and the big event on everyone's mind was the Lindbergh trial. Aviation hero Charles Lindbergh and his wife had endured the tragic kidnapping of their son, and then, several years after the body had been found, a suspect was finally arrested. Naturally, New York stations covered the trial intensely. But the trouble with covering a trial was the long periods of time when there just wasn't any interesting material worth broadcasting. Block, remembering what Al Jarvis had done so successfully, proposed to his bosses at WNEW a new and interesting way of filling the time. When the station said okay, he went out and purchased a large number of phonograph records (since WNEW didn't have any), making sure to concentrate on the biggest artists of the day. In February of 1935, New Yorkers first heard Martin Block's new show, "The Make-Believe Ballroom." It was an immediate success, so much so that it would soon have a waiting list of sponsors eager to advertise. In its heyday, "The Make-Believe Ballroom" received 12,000 pieces of fan mail a month. It didn't take long for the music publishers and song pluggers to realize this was no passing phase: Martin Block was hot, and so was his show. Exposure on that show could make a song a hit. Suddenly, there was an actual relationship between song pluggers and a radio announcer. Block welcomed this, in fact, and not for any potential free gifts: he was a student of the industry, and he thought his audience might be interested in the behind the scenes goings on, the hard work that made a song a hit. So, he began inviting various pluggers and songwriters to appear on his show and discuss their jobs, as well as promoting their songs directly to the audience. As radio's purists looked on in horror (a show where no live music was played was truly a sign of society's ultimate ruin), Martin Block became a celebrity. His concept was a huge success: WNEW made money, many new records were exposed to an eager public, and the idea of disc jockeying proved it had vast potential. Unfortunately, no trend ensued immediately. Martin Block was a few years ahead of his time. But some of his innovations would be used by Top-40 and album-rock radio years later; Block popularized the practice known today as the *miniconcert* or the *block party*, where a station plays a popular artist's or group's music in a 15-minute segment, and then does the same with another group, and another, and so on. Like his mentor, Al Jarvis, Martin Block listened to his audience, and by giving them exactly what they wanted to hear, he earned their loyalty.

What was important about both Al Jarvis and Martin Block was their great influence in helping songs to become hits. If record companies had been reluctant to support radio because they had failed to see what good it would do for their performers, now they had some definite proof. Even though radio didn't immediately clone Martin Block in cities all over the United States, he remained a major figure in New York for years, and New York was the heart of the music industry.

Meanwhile, the music industry expanded even further. There were more record labels, more publishers, more bands, and of course more song pluggers. There were also a few attempts to do away with the payment system, which was still very much alive and well. Smaller record companies resented the fact that the big companies could afford to bring gifts and cash to certain band leaders and performers in exchange for performing the right song. These smaller companies felt they were being forced out, and they tried to get the government to intervene, saying that payment of gratuities in exchange for giving a song extra exposure restricted competition, and as such, it was an unfair labor practice. But the government evidently didn't feel it had enough evidence at that time to prove a crime had been committed, plus the companies that were making the charges weren't exactly objective. The Music Publishers' Protective Association (MPPA), which had tried and failed in 1917 to eliminate bribery in the industry, failed again in 1935. The payment system continued.

The industry had other problems too: ASCAP wanted to raise their rates again and charge radio even more, largely to help offset huge losses that Hollywood was suffering. Radio, obviously, wasn't too happy about having to pay more fees to ASCAP, especially to support the movie business, but it seemed inevitable. (In case you wonder what movies had to do with ASCAP, Hollywood had helped many musicians earn a living in good times, thanks to the popularity of musicals. Now that business had slowed down, Hollywood expected ASCAP to help them out, as they felt they had helped ASCAP members whom they had provided with considerable work in the past. ASCAP evidently saw the logic in this, and went after the one industry that was doing very well: radio.) This time, however, radio wasn't about to give up without a fight. The National Association of Broadcasters (NAB) had been gathering strength, and many new members, throughout the 1930s. When ASCAP told radio of a planned 70% fee increase, the NAB said no. But they did more than just refuse to pay—they set a chain of events in motion that led to the rise of *format* radio (that is, stations that played different types of music for different audiences, such as Top-40, Black, Country, and others). First, they helped to form an alternative music licensing company to give ASCAP its first real competition. The company was called Broadcast Music Incorporated (BMI), and it took on the challenge immediately.

Before you start asking what BMI has to do with disc jockeys, and what any of this has to do with music directing, let me explain. The industry that we know today has its roots in certain innovations of the early 1900s, as we have seen. But it also has its roots in certain struggles and controversies. The fight against ASCAP made it possible for an entirely new generation of songwriters and artists to be heard on radio for the first time. Rightly or wrongly, ASCAP had become the voice of Tin Pan Alley's establishment, that is, the mostly white, conservative males who comprised its majority. ASCAP members tended to prefer traditional and serious music; few members were black, few wrote songs that were outside the middle-class mainstream. To be fair, ASCAP's purpose, that of making sure songwriters and performers received the royalties to which they were entitled, was a noble one. But ASCAP had definitely grown more conservative over the years, and its membership didn't seem to like or understand the music of young people. BMI changed all this. As a new and upstart organization, BMI's membership was often young, and it was made up of composers who hadn't fit in with ASCAP. Some were black, some were female, some wrote jazz or country songs. Some were quite talented; others were lucky to have a job. But when radio said no to ASCAP, they had to rely on BMI. Suddenly, in January of 1941, music on radio changed dramatically. Now that radio was no longer allowed to use ASCAP songs (which were the pop hits of the day), the opportunity presented itself to build some new hits. Radio had some interesting new choices, and they had to utilize them. So it was that in many cities, country and jazz and blues were heard on radio, just as they had been played on jukeboxes in years past. To many people's surprise, there didn't seem to be wholesale rebellion, partly because World War II was going on and most folks had more important things to worry about, but also because some of this new music was quite enjoyable for the audience. By the time an industry strike was settled in October of 1941, it was too late to pretend this music didn't exist. Although some radio stations returned to basically safe white pop music, others slowly began incorporating Black music into their programming, as we shall see, while Country (which had always been popular in the South) gained some new friends up north.

But the problems for the music industry weren't over yet. Just as ASCAP was counting its losses and getting used to the idea of BMI, yet another labor dispute that affected radio and records occurred. This time it came from the American Federation of Musicians (AF of M), and was fueled by the union's controversial and volatile president, James Petrillo. Petrillo had a longstanding grudge against radio: for obvious reasons, he wanted only live musicians at each station; when stations played records or tried to replace studio musicians with smaller groups, or even changed from an orchestra to just one instrument for background and mood music, it made him furious. He also disliked jukeboxes for the same reason, and he didn't see the benefit of records. All he saw was the possibility of his members losing their jobs, and he was determined to stand up for them. In fairness, he was only trying to do what he felt was right. But his methods won him few friends. Petrillo was so rigid, for example, that he opposed amateur bands and wanted even junior high school students to join the union if they wanted to play; he also felt school plays should only use union musicians. He wanted radio and record companies to pay the AF of M fees over and above what they already paid to ASCAP (and now BMI).

Needless to say, the idea wasn't greeted with enthusiasm, so the AF of M went on strike in 1942. Petrillo announced that until his demands were met, none of his musicians would play or perform anywhere. As you can imagine, this had a chilling effect on the music industry: with no musicians, how could new songs be recorded? And how could radio have the latest hits, either live or on record? The union was powerful, and few musicians would dare disobey Petrillo's orders. The President himself even requested a swift end to this madness, so that musicians could resume entertaining U.S. soldiers fighting in the war, but Petrillo and the AF of M refused. Meanwhile, some singers, frustrated with the work stoppage, went on the air anyway and sang without musicians, or they used the one instrument Petrillo had somehow overlooked, the harmonica. But while singers could wait out the strike and make do in some fashion, record companies were in deep trouble. Radio could at least play the older songs, but record companies depended on new material to keep the older material selling and to keep the fans happy. Now, no options existed.

If James Petrillo's intent was to single-handedly stop the trend away from live music, he almost succeeded. People were in fact extremely upset about the strike, disc jockeys had nothing new and exciting to share with their audience, and record companies and jukeboxes lost large sums of money while the AF of M waited for the tide to turn. Finally, it did. In 1943, Decca Records and several of the smaller companies gave in and agreed to pay the fees the AF of M wanted. The rest of the record companies held out until November of 1944, but ultimately, they too had to give in. The fees that had to be paid totaled $4,000,000 a year. It was quite a victory for Petrillo and the Union. As for Mr. Petrillo, he wasn't quite finished. He next wanted radio to employ Union members as *platter turners*, technicians whose only job was to put the records on the turntable (the disc jockey was not supposed to touch what could be considered technical equipment). This new plan would not sit well with another union, NABET (National Association of Broadcast Engineers and Technicians) who felt that only their members should be platter turners, not AF of M musicians who were between jobs. This turf war would be fought in a number of cities, with both unions fighting for control while the disc jockeys wondered what all the furor was about. Petrillo also decided that AF of M musicians wouldn't perform on any FM stations unless the AM hired a duplicate orchestra to play on the AM. (FM was still in its fledgling stages, and most AM stations simply used their FMs to simulcast AM programming; ironically, by the 1980s, it would be exactly the opposite in many cities) By this time, the broadcasters were so outraged by what they saw as excessive demands and bullying tactics that they sought relief from Congress. In 1946, they got it—the Lea Act, which gave broadcasters protection against being forced to hire unnecessary personnel or paying twice for the same service. This time Mr. Petrillo had pushed his luck. Stations faced with the order to use two orchestras or none at all were voting for none at all, as now that the strike was over, there were records again. While the Lea Act was being passed, many of these stations just eliminated studio musicians once and for all, the very thing Petrillo had been fighting. Perhaps stations might have done this sooner or later, since keeping an orchestra was a great expense, especially at the smaller stations; but when these stations were told they *had to* keep an orchestra on the payroll, and then hire a second one, it was the last straw. It was also the excuse that many stations needed. The Lea Act gave them the legal protection, and the bad feelings generated by the strike made it easier for owners to cut their orchestras from the budget. Many stations had resented Petrillo's attitude and his methods, but felt they were in no position to do anything about it until the record companies settled with the Union. By the late 1940s, only a few major market stations still had orchestras; more and more stations were relying on records and disc jockeys.

While musicians were fighting against records, another major event was taking place, one that would change radio even more dramatically. It had not been until early 1940 that radio stations won the right to play records without restrictions: up until then, stations were required to make periodic announcements that, in effect, apologized for the fact that this was a record and not a live concert. (People like Martin Block got around this by calling their show the "Make-Believe Ballroom," but the truth was that most people no longer felt live music was better, if in fact they ever did). Then, just when more stations had begun using records and the disc jockey became more common (not always for noble reasons—it was chapter for a station to hire a DJ and buy some records than to have an announcer and a succession of live bands, each with its own vocalists), new competition arose and threatened to make radio obsolete.

Television had been around in an experimental phase for a few years, but it took off in the late 1940s. Suddenly, major radio stars defected in large numbers to this new medium. The radio networks were hurting, the Golden Age of Radio had reached an abrupt end, and people who had listened avidly to soap operas or dramas on radio were now sitting in front of their TV sets watching these shows come to life. Naturally, the common wisdom was that radio was finished. However, as it turned out, radio was just starting to embark on an entirely different venture, for an entirely new audience—teenagers. No one knew this yet, for these postwar baby boomers had just been born. In a very quiet way, signs of change were showing up. In 1946, the clock radio was first put on the market, by General Electric. It was a huge success, as people much preferred waking up to radio than to TV. Car radios also benefited from some new and improved technology—early models had been ugly and unreliable. By the mid-1940s, that was no longer a problem, and over nine million automobiles had a radio in them. Where TV was fine for in-home viewing, radio became an excellent entertainment source for people riding to and from work each day. By 1953, another major innovation, the transistor radio, made radio truly portable. Despite the inroads that television made, radio did not die—it simply carved out its particular niche and continued to serve its audience. But what about that event that changed radio so dramatically? No, I wasn't referring to the rise of television, although that certainly had an impact on radio, nor to advances like clock radios or transistors. The event that started a major trend probably passed unnoticed back then, just as the births of all those baby boomers did at the time. But later on, many people understood how important it was that day in 1948 when WDIA appeared.

WDIA in Memphis was an unlikely trendsetter. It had a weak signal, and was only licensed to operate during daytime hours. But its influence and its impact would be massive. WDIA was the first station to have all-black announcers and to play all-black music. Other stations before WDIA had played black music, especially rhythm and blues (R & B)—this often happened during the ASCAP, strike but the majority of stations that tried to program R & B had white announcers. Also, it still was not considered a wise programming strategy to aim exclusively at blacks. Stereotypes prevailed, and it was felt that advertisers would never support such a station. WDIA proved the common wisdom wrong. Although owned by white men, WDIA called itself "The Mother Station of the Negroes." Its air staff featured two music legends, Riley "B.B." King and Rufus "Bear Cat" Thomas, as well as Martha Jean "the Queen" Steinberg (a black woman with five kids, married to a Jewish musician, who one day decided she wanted a career in radio and went on to become a major success). Although a small station, WDIA soon proved that it could sell its sponsors' products quite effectively. It also was very effective at selling records. The announcers (*disc jockey* was still not a commonly used term in the late 40s) picked their own music. Rufus Thomas, who didn't officially join WDIA until 1950, had already made a name for himself in Memphis as a musician, dancer, and host of a local talent show. He loved the blues, and eventually made a number of records; such rock superstars as the Rolling Stones name him as one of their musical influences. In addition to being called Bear Cat (and having a hit record by that name), Thomas is also known as the "Daddy of Memphis Soul." As for B.B. King, the former jingle singer has had a long and illustrious career in blues, and he too influenced many later rock stars. Suffice it to say the air staff of WDIA understood Memphis, could relate well to their listeners, and helped WDIA maintain an up-to-date-image. This was not a station programmed for older people. It played the best R & B, and even experimented with fast-talking announcers. The station's unofficial mentor was Nat D. Williams, or "Nat Dee" as he called himself on his popular show, "Tan Town Jamboree." A former Memphis high school teacher, it was he who encouraged many young blacks to get into radio, Rufus Thomas among them. Nat Williams may not have become a recording star, but he was one of the South's first black announcers, and the airplay he provided helped launch numerous hit records. By the early 1950s, WDIA had a power increase, and was a financial success.

Meanwhile, in Nashville, a station with a much bigger signal had been making its own impact, although in a slightly different way. WLAC had been playing R & B on a limited scale since the early 1940s, one of the first basically white stations to do so. In fact, WLAC had what would to us be a rather schizoid programming philosophy. By day, WLAC played Country plus some traditional white pop, of the Tin Pan Alley variety. But late at night, it miraculously changed into the premier location on the dial for the best Black hits. Because WLAC had such an excellent signal, especially at night, it could be heard in a number of states, and was directly responsible for introducing black music to white audiences. Contrary to the popular stereotypes that whites would never accept black music, large numbers of white young adults found WLAC and loved what they heard. Also, contrary to the commonly held belief that most blacks were poor and as such not a desirable audience for sponsors, large numbers of WLAC's audience came from a newly emerging black middle- and upper-middle class. Much of this was centered around Fisk University, where black college students kept the white air staff of WLAC aware of the newest R & B records. But the WLAC announcers were not opportunists. The fact was that although they were white, DJs Gene Nobles, Hoss Allen, and John R. genuinely enjoyed rhythm and blues. On the down side, some white parents weren't pleased about this new type of music their children had discovered. The songs seemed to have suggestive and often overtly sexual lyrics, for one thing. For another, one of the announcers, Gene Nobles, liked to make off-color comments and was a master of double entendres. Yet even when local ministers threatened to call the FCC and demand that WLAC's license be revoked, management stood by its staff and their choice of music. In fact, WLAC's outrageous image was probably seen as an asset by the many young people who listened. Meanwhile the announcers were doing countless testimonials,. for everything from black hair-care products to diet pills to baby chicks. They also helped a local record-store owner sell huge numbers of records when he finally decided to advertise on WLAC. That owner, Randy Wood, later went on to become a record company president and a multimillionaire, but it was his initial venture as a sponsor on Gene Nobles's show (his first commercial ran at midnight) that convinced him of the power of both WLAC and R & B music. In addition to playing the newest songs (some so new they hadn't even been released yet, and the record companies were just testing them to see if they had any hit potential), Gene, Hoss, and John R. interviewed popular black musicians. They also were performers themselves—not musicians, but their shows were flashy, entertaining and had high energy at a time when announcers still spoke seriously at the vast majority of stations. Each had his own persona and used it well.

The late 1940s saw many stations begin to play Black music late at night. Many stations hired jive-talking personalities with names like Poppa Stoppa or Doctor Daddy-o or even Dizzy Lizzy. One very popular R & B announcer in Austin, Texas, called himself Doctor Hepcat and spoke in a language only those in the know could follow. Suddenly, the influence of R & B was everywhere. And soon, it would take on a new form, *rock and roll.*

4

Formats Come into Their Own

As we have observed in previous chapters, the music industry was still growing. It had survived and prospered through two world wars, the Great Depression, and the emergence of television. Whether the economy was good or bad, whether people stayed home or went out to socialize, the one constant was the popularity of music, be it on radio, in jukeboxes, in clubs, or on records. The styles changed, the dance crazes changed, the big stars changed; but the music industry kept growing, overcoming labor disputes, critics who hated popular music, and whatever other obstacles seemed certain to destroy it. In fact, by the 1940s, the way record promotion was done was more complex than ever, and there were more people doing it.

Today, as we will discuss in more detail later, record companies use a two-pronged attack to create a hit. One part of that attack is planned by the company's home office (which is usually in Los Angeles or New York for pop music, and Nashville for Country), where vice presidents of promotion decide which records will be given the biggest promotional push and plan exactly how the records will be promoted. The implementation of that plan occurs at the local level in each major city, where companies have branch offices. At the branch, the local promoters receive their copies of the particular record, which nowadays is more often a CD or cassette, as well as whatever promotional items go with it (posters, for example), and then begin the process of visiting stations, calling them, or both to convince the program and music directors that they should add one of these new releases.

As the music industry moved into the years just before rock music, a pecking order had developed. It was no longer just the music publishers and the song pluggers: the industry was too big for that, and there were too many stations. Not all song pluggers were dishonest, nor did they all use money to get their songs selected. Many were creative, unique individuals with a flair for drama. They knew how to get a band leader' attention, and they knew how to win the trust of a performer. The idea of promoting was still directed at getting the right song to the right artist, although with more records available, there was now another dimension to the song plugger's work—making sure the record was heard by the public, which meant seeking out Martin Block and other DJs and playing the record for them.

Sheet music was still selling, although it was no longer the configuration of choice. It was obvious that the young people, who now seemed fascinated by a type of dance music called *be-bop*, were going to continue being a major force in shaping the industry's future. These young adults didn't generally gather around the piano to sing; they liked to dance and they liked to hear the hits, whether performed live or on records. Since the days when eager fans called *bobby-soxers* expressed their adoration of Frank Sinatra (and other singers considered good looking), young people had become frequent purchasers of records. Finding a teen idol to sing a given song would certainly help the song become a hit (a phenomenon we still see today); getting the song to be played on an important disc jockey's show was equally important. There were also weekly countdown shows: the best known in the 1940s was probably the network show "Your Hit Parade," which ranked the songs in order of popularity once a week.

As record promotion evolved, the song pluggers were given a new name, to express their increased responsibility. They were called *contact men*. (Yes, they were mostly always men; record promotion was seen as a male occupation in those days, undoubtedly because promoters had to keep late hours and visit band leaders or performers in clubs that weren't always in the best neighborhoods, and it was felt back then that women would not be safe in such a job, nor would it give them time for what was felt to be their primary role, caring for their family. It wouldn't be until the *1980s* that women would finally break through this sexism and earn more jobs in the record business.)

In addition to the contact man, there were his various assistants who went out with him or helped behind the scenes in organizing what calls and visits needed to be made. Overseeing what the contact man did was the general professional manager, who was in charge of the song plugging department which every Tin Pan Alley publishing house had. The job of the professional manager was somewhat similar to what record companies today call artists and repertoire directing (A & R); it was this person who chose what songs the publishing house would accept and promote (whereas today, the A & R director is responsible for scouting potential new talent and then getting that talent signed to a contract with the record company). Once the professional manager had decided on a song, he was then responsible for finding the right performer to record it and getting it signed to a major record label. (Today, while some A & R people still match songs up with singers, the majority of groups in pop music have their own original material that they want to record, and those who do not are put in touch with established songwriters to help them find a potential hit.)

During those more complex times in the 1940s, as records outpaced sheet music and young people began dominating the purchase of records, the plugger or contact man still carried copies of the sheet music, because the performers and bandleaders would need them. But eventually, he also carried recordings, which were often in the form of *demos*. A demo was a rough version of a song, which a singer had gone into the studio and performed in order to get an idea of how it might sound. This demo was not for sale to the public yet; it was mainly for the purpose of getting important people's opinions about whether or not the song had any hit potential. If enough bandleaders or disc jockeys liked a demo (the word was the abbreviated form of *demonstration*), the singer would go back into the studio and do a more polished version that would be released on record. Demos were also used to show bandleaders how good a song might sound if their own famous lead vocalist performed it; often several versions of the same song would become popular. This practice, called *covering* a song, appeared repeatedly in the 1950s, when white artists would do a version of a black hit: despite the new opportunities the AFTRA strike opened up for black music in the 1940s and early 50s, there was still a stereotype at many white stations about music that sounded "too black." When that occurred, record companies would choose a popular white performer to record a version of the song that would supposedly be more accessible for white audiences. More about this will be said later.

Meanwhile, the 1940s were ending and this new societal phenomenon of teenagers as music consumers was fascinating both to the music industry representatives (who would be affected by it) and sociologists (who just wanted to understand it better). These teens had their own particular musical preferences, their own styles, even their own language. They seemed to conform to each other, and music was what held them together. One sociologist went so far as to do interviews with a number of teens, most of whom were not too good at articulating the deep, philosophical reasons for their love of pop music. Still, as David Riesman wrote in 1950, although the typical young fan, who was now part of the majority of radio listeners, had no idea who sang most of the songs, it didn't seem to matter. As long as the song was considered a hit, this person was happy. Some of these teenagers did have a favorite singing star, but, in general, they just liked the hits and sharing the experience of pop music with their friends. In fact, Riesman noted, "[t]he functions of music for this group are social—the music gives them something to talk. . . about with friends; an opportunity to judge which tunes will become hits, couples with a lack of concern about how hits are actually made; an opportunity for identification with star singers or band leaders as 'personalities,' with little interest in. . . understanding the technologies of the radio medium itself." Riesman also noted the existence of a smaller group of young people who also loved music but knew a lot more about it, considered themselves much more musically aware than other people, thought the hits were boring, and preferred alternative or outside-the-mainstream music. These young people saw themselves as rebels with a cause: their cause was getting those boring hits off the radio and replacing them with what they felt was good music (back then, jazz and traditional blues).

What is especially interesting about Riesman's interviews is that they are still so applicable to radio listening today. Today's actives prefer listening to college radio or to other alternative stations. Music for them is still a statement and a way of life; they are proud of being nonconformists. Realizing that most of its audience was made up of these actives, one alternative rock station, WFNX in Boston, began marketing itself as "Rock the Boat Radio," or radio that wasn't afraid to break the rules. (Despite how loyal actives are to the music they love, and although they write and call and buy lots of CDs and concert tickets, they tend to comprise only about 7% of the average audience.)

As for passives, they too haven't changed much from how David Riesman described them in 1950. They love music but don't know much about it. They prefer music that is familiar (hits) and don't see themselves as crusaders. Music is their favorite form of *entertainment*; they don't analyze or critique it. They often can't tell you what station they were listening to or who sang that song you and I have heard a million times, but they are devoted to radio in their own way. Though they may not write or call, what is important about them is they still comprise over 90% of the typical station's audience.

Let's get back to the changes in the music industry and how we today are affected by them: I don't want to give the impression that radio and records were totally dominated by teenagers. Rather, having been totally dominated by adults for so many years, now the industry had split into two segments. Adults were still served by the majority of stations, which played what had come to be known as *Middle of the Road* (MOR) music. But more and more stations were seeing the trend of teens becoming important, and not wanting to appear behind the times (but also not wanting to alienate the adult audiences they already had), some stations began airing special shows that featured some of the music the teens liked. Traditional MOR stations that had for years served adults by giving them lots of news, sports, and safe, comfortable music now found it useful to do countdown shows on nights or weekends, time periods when teenagers listened more than adults. They also began taking requests and playing dedications. But what we call rock and roll was still several years away.

While there were still a few holdouts who stayed with live orchestras, by 1950 almost every radio station was playing records, and disc jockeys were fairly common. Many of the disc jockeys knew little about the teen music and simply ignored it. But others decided to make it part of their daily show. One such innovator was Ross "The Musical Boss" Miller, of MOR stronghold WTIC in Hartford. WTIC had countless awards for public service and still had programs devoted to opera and symphony. Yet, Ross Miller, who had previously been a talk-show host for the station, transformed himself into WTIC's first pop music DJ. His shift was afternoons, when the kids had just gotten out of school and wanted to hear the hits. On his new show, he was among the first northern white DJs to use jingles and rhyming slang. He became so popular with young listeners in Hartford that record companies began bringing him demos so he could decide which ones they should release to the public. The music Miller played was still not what we would consider rock, but his selections revolved around the teen idols of the day, whom he was often able to interview. As with Martin Block a few years earlier, getting Ross Miller to play a certain record could assure its becoming a hit.

Another popular announcer of this transitional era was Bob Clayton, who held down the afternoon shift at MOR powerhouse WHDH in Boston. Clayton, who ultimately left the music industry in the 1970s and returned to his original profession, practicing law, had a show called "Boston Ballroom." (Many shows with the word "ballroom" proliferated because young listeners enjoyed music they could dance to.) Like Ross Miller, and a growing number of other influential DJs (including Eddie Hubbard of WIND in Chicago, Kurt Webster of WBT in Charlotte, Joe Niagara of WIBG in Philadelphia, and Hunter Hancock who worked for several Los Angeles stations), Bob Clayton realized that the future of the industry was the young people, and he was determined to include them in his audience. Since the end of the AF of M strike, big band music had been on the decline: the unintended result of musicians being forced to sit out the music scene for a long time was that by the time they returned, the scene had shifted from big bands to star vocalists. Now, in the early 1950s, the key for any successful DJ was to blend the hits the adults had loved in the 40s with the new hits the younger audience wanted. Fortunately, some of the new hits also appealed to the older adults, so it was possible to maintain both audiences.

This would be true until rock and roll took over and helped to create stations exclusively for teens.

As was still common in the early 1950s, the DJs chose their own music. They also talked with the record promoters from each of the major record companies, because now that records had become so popular with young people, a new emphasis was being placed on promoting records at radio stations. Bob Clayton didn't have the benefit of research which today's PDs and MDs derive from a large number of informational publications known as *the trades*. These music industry magazines today include *Billboard, Hits, Monday Morning Replay, Variety, Pop Music Survey, Friday morning Quarterback*, and many more. Trade publications have industry news and gossip, discuss the latest trends, and give the playlists of a number of important radio stations; they also compile a weekly chart of the biggest-selling records nationally. Along with the music industry newspaper, *Radio & Records* (known as R & R), these publications offer the PD and MD a vast amount of useful data about all the current hits, as well as predications about what the next hits will be. Bob Clayton worked during a time when there were not only very few trades, but the ones at his disposal didn't concentrate only on radio; they devoted just as much space to movies, theater, and jukeboxes as they did to the latest trends in music. So, he looked at *Billboard* and *Variety*, but mainly, he relied on his own instincts to determine what songs his audience might like, and he confirmed his feelings with whatever listener response he received when he played a new song.

Also around this time, record stores were assuming a more important role in the hit-making process. For years, there had been a few retail outlets that stocked large inventories of records and did a sizable mail-order business to cities where no record stores existed. But with the emergence of young people as a record-buying force, more record stores opened u. Many of these stores became places where the teens would congregate and listen to the new releases (stores back then allowed a customer to do this, prior to purchasing a record). Store managers, who of course wanted to be up to date and stock the right records, made friends with the important DJs so that if a song was getting lots of radio reaction, the store could make sure copies were available for sale. Ironically, back then the stores called radio stations, whereas today, so-calledÈ *store research* entails PDs or MDs calling stores to find out what their big sellers are.

Bob Clayton, like other DJs of the early 1950s, was able to have a direct relationship with the audience. Since there were still no official rules about how to execute a format, he was free to do whatever he felt would please his listeners. For example, if he played a song and many listeners immediately called to say they liked it, he would play it again right away (whereas today's formatic rules, called *rotations*, assign specific play times and seldom if ever allow the same song to be repeated until its rotation comes up; for example, the No. 1 song might be in a rotation that repeats every 75 minutes, but not before. Because of his influence on the Boston music scene, soon Clayton was being given advance copies of songs so that he could play them first; needless to say, the other stations in town were not amused. He also found himself being invited out to dinner by various promoters and publishers, but he didn't go. As he recalls, he decided it wasn't a good idea to socialize with people who were trying to influence how he programmed his show; because he wanted to program it objectively, he didn't want friendships to play any part. As a result of this, Clayton developed a reputation for scrupulous honesty. In fact, during the payola scandals a few years later, other Boston DJs were found guilty, but Bob Clayton was found to have had absolutely no involvement.

Very few stations had a person called a music director at that time, although a few did have some rules about what songs would be played. At WHDH, the rules prior to the payola scandal mainly involved what live music the station would play and during whose show. There was a music director, who was really a member of the station's morning team but whose job consisted mostly of booking the live performers and making sure they had what they needed to perform. A number of stations did have a music librarian, however. This person, who was often female and from the secretarial ranks, was responsible for keeping the library in order. In the days of all-live music, the job wasn't necessary, but now that records were so important, most stations had begun acquiring a large number of them. The music librarian filed and catalogued the records so that the DJs could find the ones they were looking for. Also, the librarian maintained contact with all the record companies so that scratchy copies could be replaced promptly. In the early 1950s this wasn't difficult to do, since there were only four major record companies that accounted for the majority of all record sales—Columbia, RCA Victor, Decca, and Capitol as well as a few small independents. But as far as choosing the music, that was still up to the disc jockey. At some stations, the music librarian was very knowledgeable, and DJs might ask for an opinion or a suggestion. But in general, at that time, working in the music library required good organizational skills more than a knowledge of music.

As I mentioned earlier, many young people depended on shows such as "Your Hit Parade" to tell them what the week's biggest hits were. This show, the forerunner of all countdowns, first aired as a network radio show in 1935. It was sponsored by Lucky Strike cigarettes, and it was at the sponsor's office each week that the list of hits was compiled. From what we know about the research methods of the 1930s, we may assume the list wasn't very scientific; it may have even been helped along by a few hard-working song pluggers. No one would explain what criteria were used to determine a song's position on that week's list, but getting a song onto "Your Hit Parade" became one of the song plugger's most important missions. Since the trades didn't start publishing their own lists of hits until as late as the mid-40s, "Your Hit Parade" was the most visible proof a song plugger had that his record was really a hit (and the more of a hit it was, the more famous performers would want to use it). Because there were only ten songs chosen each week on the show, the competition must have been intense. Audiences waited expectantly every Saturday night as they tried to guess what the new No. 1 hit was. The show enjoyed great success until the rock era. Why did rock and roll cause "Your Hit Parade" to end? Actually, television played part too, and rock just finished the job. While "Your Hit Parade" was on radio, it dominated, largely because its concept was perfect for radio. The show did not translate well to TV: the cast was much more comfortable on radio, and critics said they performed like robots in front of a TV camera. Also, on radio, all they had to do was sing the song, whereas on TV, they had to act it out or do something to keep people interested (the same problem that song slides had many years earlier). But the real problem for "Your Hit Parade" involved major change in attitudes. In the 1930s and 40s, people had been artist-oriented. They didn't care who sang the song, as long as it was somebody famous. When rock and roll caught on, its fans didn't want to hear the cast of "Your Hit Parade" singing the hits: they wanted the original artists, just like they had heard on their favorite station. Unknown singers doing Elvis Presley's music just wouldn't do: it had to be Elvis or nobody. Eventually, it was nobody, because the show died a merciful death. But we owe "Your Hit Parade" a debt of gratitude for proving that playing the hits in order of importance, and creating a suspenseful atmosphere while making the audience wait for that No. 1 song was a winning concept; it is still used with great success and has made such countdown hosts as Casey Kasem very wealthy.

Sometime between the years 1949 and 1954 (depending on whose version of the story you hear), one of radio's turning points occurred. Just as KDIA's success playing Black music was an important moment in the development of what we know as formats, so was the day Todd Storz decided to take his friend, PD Bill Stewart, out for a beer. The two became involved in a discussion, so the story goes, and sat around the local pub for hours talking. While there, Storz, who owned station KOWH in Omaha, observed a waitress periodically going over to the jukebox, where she played the same song over and over. Suddenly it occurred to Storz: radio was ignoring a fundamental truth about its audience by not repeating hit songs. People did want to hear their favorites more than once. (Back in the pre-rock days, it was common for the DJs, who picked their own music, to play a wide variety. MOR stations in particular believed people wanted to hear different songs every day, and although they might play a certain big hit on consecutive days, most stations avoided repetition as much as they could.) But Storz realized that familiarity wasn't a bad thing to the listener, and if the song was popular, it could definitely be played again. From this realization (which jukebox owners could have told him years earlier) came what we know today as Contemporary Hit Radio, (CHR) which was first known as Top-40.

Top-40's name may have changed over the years, but its concept is much the same as when Todd Storz and Bill Stewart implemented it on KOWH in the early 1950s. Storz put in a specific playlist of songs and set up the rotations such that the biggest hits would repeat very frequently (the No. 1 song was repeated hourly); he also chose a "pick hit of the week," a song he and Bill felt had hit potential. It was an idea whose time had come—radio as a jukebox—and was in marked contrast to MOR, where no one song received any more play than any other. In its original form, there were no Oldies (for obvious reasons—the format was brand new), just between 30 and 40 hits played over and over. It was hit radio, nothing but the hits, and it was heavily influenced by requests (and, no doubt, by quick-thinking record promoters, who knew a good idea when they saw one).

Not long after Todd Storz began his first attempts at Top-40 in Omaha, another radio innovator, Gordon McLendon of KLIF in Dallas began a version of his own, with one added element: outrageous promotions and contests. McLendon brought his show-business flair to radio, designing publicity stunts that would get his station noticed and talked about, while he continued to entertain the audience. For example, he would send his DJs out to unusual locations (telephone booths, street corners) to do remotes. One time, he sent a "mystery millionaire" around Dallas handing out

$20 bills. McLendon wasn't afraid to be different at a time when radio stations in general still maintained a formal and conservative approach.

KLIF in its early days wasn't really a Top-40; it was a Top-25. That was all McLendon felt a station needed—25 top hits, rotated all the time. Evidently he was right because KLIF became a major success. What is especially interesting about McLendon and Storz is that they both realized something about the audience's listening habits that has become a truism today but was revolutionary back then. They noticed that their young listeners would tune in for a while, tune out, and tune back in. . . . they didn't listen continuously, although the station may have been on in the background the entire time. What made them listen closely was hearing a favorite song. Thus, it was especially important for a successful station to play those big hit songs often. Perhaps older adults might find this close repetition annoying, but for the younger listeners, it was perfect. To this day, successful stations aimed at young listeners make sure the top hits, often called *Power* records or *Hots* are frequently replayed, knowing as they do that this audience is impatient about hearing its favorite songs and doesn't want to wait too long.

If you looked back at *Billboard Magazine*'s charts to see what the top hits were in the early 1950s, you would have seen the transition occurring. A number of big-signal stations, among them WLAC in Nashville, were having success playing the adult music during the day and the younger music (including some of the black hit songs) at night. But the charts still reflected a Tin Pan Alley, traditional white pop orientation until about 1954, when, slowly, certain black songs began to *cross over*, that is, become hits with the mainstream pop audience. Black singers had had hits with white audiences in the past, but these singers, such as Nat "King" Cole, performed mainly pop music and were considered safe by white programmers. Now, black groups whose roots were in rhythm and blues were gaining sufficient exposure on radio to create growing sales of their records among white teenagers. While it wasn't so in every market, it was enough of a factor that musically aware disc jockeys who wanted to attract the teen audience at night began adding more R & B into their music mix.

Naturally, music critics regarded R & B the same way that previous generations of writers had regarded ragtime and jazz. Not all critics condemned it; some even liked it. But the majority felt that R & B was inferior to the music of the Tin Pan Alley tradition. Some racist sentiments emerged in some of the complaints about R & B music, with the usual comments about it being "jungle music" and, of course, obscene. Time, however, was marching on, and R & B was more than a fad; it was a musical genre whose moment had arrived. More Black stations had emerged since WDIA proved there was a profit to be made with that format. R & B was being heard in more cities, yet on mainstream pop radio, it was as if R & B didn't exist. This trend just didn't fit in with MOR radio's style, said program directors, explaining why they weren't playing any R & B. It was too harsh, too strident, the audience would be offended. Meanwhile, a number of white musicians were getting their first opportunities to hear R & B, and they became influenced by its energy; one singer who faithfully listened to R & B on WDIA grew up to make quite an impact on the music industry: his name was Elvis Presley, and his moment had arrived too.

It is almost impossible to pinpoint the exact beginning of Rock and Roll. The name, however, is credited to DJ Alan Freed, who borrowed it from several blues songs ("to rock" and "to roll" were popular euphemisms for sexual intercourse, although I also heard "to rock" was a slang expression for partying). Freed, who became one of the first full-time rock DJs, began his career doing news and also worked at a classical station. It was in Akron, Ohio, in the late 1940s that he became a popular teen-oriented announcer. In 1951, he moved to Cleveland, and despite a problem with alcohol (a problem that steadily worsened over the years), he started a popular late-night R & B program called "The Moon Dog Show." Thanks in large part to the sponsorship of a local record store owner, Leo Mintz, who had been observing all the white kids buying black records. Ironically, black adults of the early 50s were experiencing a backlash against R & B—these older adults preferred gospel, and felt R & B had strayed too far from God. The black kids, like the white kids, felt R & B was theirs, and no matter how many parents accused it of being "the devil's music," they remained devoted to it. As for Alan Freed, he knew the young white adults couldn't relate to Big Bands and didn't understand jazz. Rhythm and blues was perfect for them; it was up-tempo and easy to dance to. Freed knew how to talk in that special language that black announcers used; he could talk it so effectively that many blacks in his audience were amazed to learn he was white. Although it may sound somewhat condescending to say a white announcer could talk like a black, bear in mind that there was an actual *style* of jiving, rhyming, and rapping that was used at R & B stations, and it was emulated by both white announcers who respected it and new black announcers who wanted to sound like their heroes. Freed became the Moon Dog, and his popularity with his young fans grew. In 1952, he held what many regard as the first rock concert, an event he called Moon Dog's Coronation Ball, and what it lacked in big-name talent it made up for in hype. The arena held 10,000; as many as 7,000 more showed up to try to get in. The majority of the attendees were black, although some whites did attend, and the overcrowding led to several fights and the police being summoned. The concert was canceled; the newspapers all said it was a disgrace, and the publicity made Freed determined to hold another concert very soon. He switched to smaller-hall concerts, and before long, his shows were a fixture in and around Cleveland, with an increasingly more equal blend of black and white fans in attendance.

Cleveland was a good example of the newly emerging power of the disc jockey and his ability to make records hits. Among the popular DJs in the early 1950s were Joe Finan, Soupy Sales, and Bill Randall, all of whom worked at pop-oriented stations; only Alan Freed played R & B exclusively; as he was now in a more important air-shift, not just restricted to late nights, his popularity grew. With all these important announcers making decisions about what songs their audience would hear, the record companies wasted no time sending their promoters to visit the DJs and play the new releases for them.

While Alan Freed was a master at getting publicity, Bill Randall was a master at anticipating new trends, especially those that would appeal to his established pop audience and yet bring in new listeners. It was he who first broke such popular vocalists as Johnny Ray (an extremely dramatic singer whose stage act often involved his breaking into tears in the midst of a sad song), the Crew-Cuts, and a then-unknown southern singer named Elvis. Randall didn't personally like much of the new music (neither did Bob Clayton), but he knew a hit when he heard one, and his shows received high ratings.

As Cleveland's DJs fought to play the new hits first, Alan Freed set his sights on bigger markets. His personal problems hadn't improved, but he was an exciting air personality, and by 1954 he was hired full time by WINS in New York. Freed began referring to *rock and roll* on the air—at that time it had no official name, although in Texas it was known as *cat music*—and he set in motion the events that made him famous (and ultimately destroyed his career).

At that time, New York was still dominated by the traditional MOR stations. Once Freed established himself in the 7 to 11 P.M. shift, there was no stopping him. He filled a void in the market, and the kids loved him. Although he couldn't call himself the Moon Dog (New York already had one), and although some members of the black media found his act offensive (they felt he was taking a job away from a black DJ and accused him of being little more than an opportunist, earning his living at the expense of black musicians), he quickly acquired a large following of both black and white kids. Freed actually was doing radio at a perfect time: TV had pretty much eliminated the power of the radio networks, which opened the door for local radio; and many local stations began to rely heavily on *personalities*, announcers who were also entertainers, performers, and unique characters. Freed was a bit of all these, but in the radio industry overall, the mid-50s were becoming the era of the disc jockey.

Even the magazine often referred to as the "Bible," *Billboard*, stated that the disc jockey was now "the undisputed king of local radio programming." What were these newly crowned kings doing with their fame? In an article about what the typical DJ did in addition to talking about records, Billboard noted that DJs could also be found "owning record stores, making personal appearances, songwriting, managing artists, publishing music, and operating jukebox routes." Billboard noted that in Los Angeles, the most popular DJs also promoted concerts and local dances. If any of this seems like conflicts of interest to you, remember that the payola hearings hadn't happened yet, and rock was still a new event for radio. New events seldom have firmly established rules, as you may recall from radio's early days. In fairness to some of the early rock DJs, many simply saw an opportunity and jumped in, while others possibly were dishonest and trying to make easy money. The many DJs who doubled as concert promoters or stocked jukeboxes probably saw nothing wrong with doing so. After all, what was the harm in making a few extra dollars? The songwriting credits, however, were a lot more questionable, a remnant of the old payment system from radio's earliest days, when song pluggers would give performers credit for songs they never wrote as a way to hide the fact that they wanted to give those performers payoffs in exchange for favorable consideration of those songs. Certainly, there were a few talented DJs who really did write songs, but most never wrote a note; songwriting credits were just another way for record companies to reward certain DJs and encourage their future goodwill. But this method often short-changed the artists who really did write the songs. Chuck Berry, for example, was shocked to discover his Top-5 hit from 1955, "Maybellene" had been credited to Alan Freed as co-writer, which meant Berry would have to share the royalties. It took many years, and many legal battles, before Berry was able to get any of the money he had earned from that song. Unfortunately, he was not the only one. Other musicians, many of them black, found out later that their songs had been assigned to somebody else, and they were not able to recover those royalties. (For a more detailed discussion of these unethical practices, read *Rock 'n' Roll Is Here to Pay* by Steve Chapple and Reebee Garofalo, or *Hit Men* by Fredric Dannen.)

While all this was going on, the musical preferences of the DJs were becoming more influential. *Billboard Magazine* began keeping a chart that listed the top tunes according to the *jockeys*, and also the top tunes in the jukeboxes. By 1955, many more songs in the top positions reflected the rock style, and even more were by black performers. Fats Domino, LaVern Baker, the Penguins, the Platters, and Nappy Brown could be found on the same charts that listed hits by Frank Sinatra, Perry Como, and other white pop artists. There were also even more cover versions of black songs, such as "Earth Angel," which reached No. 8 in its original by the Penguins, and No. 3 in its cover version by the white pop group, the Crew-Cuts. Perhaps the most amusing cover version is a No. 1 song from 1955 by pop vocalist Georgia Gibbs, "Dance with Me Henry." In its original incarnation, it was an R & B smash with fairly explicit lyrics, sung by Hank Ballard, "Work with Me Annie." To his credit, Alan Freed nearly always refused to play cover versions. But many stations that did use them felt the original versions had lyrics that were much too graphic, and it would thus be safer to play a clean version of the song, rather than risk offending the audience in a still conservative era. As you might expect, most young listeners didn't mind at all, but their parents were quite concerned, especially as this new music began getting bad publicity.

Many people feel that "Rock Around the Clock" was the first rock and roll song. Performed by former country and western artist Bill Haley and the Comets, it went to No. 1 in 1955, and from then on the charts began changing, moving away from Tin Pan Alley pop and toward the hist so many young people were buying. Records were changing too. They had been 78 rpm, large, cumbersome discs that broke easily and couldn't accommodate a long song. Most record companies during that pre-rock period released a limited number of recordings—perhaps 12 a year, and the head of A & R (formerly the general professional manager) made all the major decisions about which artists would record which songs when. But rock, and the demand for new records, changed that. While A & R executives still had influence, many didn't understand this new rock music. Also, some disliked it intensely and wished it would go away—Columbia's A & R chief, Mitch Miller, once berated an audience of rock DJs, accusing them of abandoning good music and making the teenager more important than was necessary. He felt teens as an audience could offer radio nothing; they had no buying power, he said, and no taste in their musical preferences, so radio was about to be ruined. Miller, who had great affinity for Tin Pan Alley music, was very wrong about the teen audience. Rather than dooming radio, teens probably rescued it. Their love for Top-40 music gave them, and an entirely new generation, a reason to choose radio over television. As for buying power, one estimate said teens alone purchased over $150 million worth of records in the mid-50s.

To accommodate the influx of young record fans, record companies found themselves scrambling to sign new groups and find new material. Atlantic Records became extremely influential with rock fans; under the leadership of Ahmet Ertegun and Jerry Wexler, this company was at the forefront of signing R & B artists and promoting their music to the rock audience. As for that music, it was now issued on 45 rpm discs, which were smaller and more compact, easy for teens to buy and collect. The 78 soon became obsolete, and the other available configuration, the 33 and 1/3 (better known as the long-playing album, or LP), became popular with adults. In the late 1960s, of course, it would become the choice of college radio and Album Rock fans, as we will see when the Album-Oriented Rock (AOR) format developed.

Another DJ (or, more accurately, a TV-J, since the records on his show were played before a TV audience) with immense influence over the hit-making process was Dick Clark, whose "American Bandstand" first appeared on TV in 1957. The show itself had been around since 1952, hosted by local Philadelphia personality Bob Horn. But its success as a national TV show can be attributed to the efforts of Dick Clark and his staff. The importance of "American Bandstand" in breaking hits was enormous, and during the payola hearing several years later, questions would be raised about whether Clark's motive for playing certain songs was because he thought they were hits or because he owned a financial interest in them. (While Clark never denied having close relationships with certain record promoters and companies and acknowledged that he sometimes received gifts out of gratitude for his having helped a certain artist, he emphatically denied that his show was for sale or that the gifts and friendships ever persuaded him to play a song he felt had no hit potential.)

The best thing about Dick Clark from a marketing standpoint (and what probably helped him to emerge relatively unscathed from the payola scandal of 1960) was his wholesome image. Not only did Clark look like the proverbial "all-American boy," but his studio audience, made up of attractive teens neatly dressed in the latest fashions, looked equally wholesome. These teens did the latest dances and rated the new songs ("It's got a good beat, and it's easy to dance to" was their highest praise). But more important, they showed American parents that rock and roll was popular with the "nice kids" and not just with the delinquents. Where Alan Freed's rock events turned into riots, Dick Clark's TV show was safe and nonthreatening to the average parent. The controversy that seemed to follow Freed (some of which was unintentional, but some of which did seem like an effort to get more publicity) was never part of Clark's persona. All across America, teenagers eager to learn the new dances and see the popular performers made "American Bandstand" a giant success. (Today, many baby boomers can still recall watching the show every day to see which couples were dancing with each other, who appeared to be in love, and who the best dancers were. The "Bandstand" teens thus became role models who transcended their original function of merely dancing to the latest hits.)

The end of the 1950s also meant the end of autonomy for the DJ; as we will see in an upcoming chapter, the payola scandal changed the way music was programmed at radio stations. In rock's early years, the typical station had some policies, but it also had "star" DJs who did what they wanted and were seldom held accountable. Before we consider how this led to payola, we should first examine what direction popular music was taking.

Top-40 and rock music had a dramatic effect on popular culture, but other formats, such as Black and Country, were also going through some transitions. As we discussed earlier, radio programming in most major cities had been dominated by

MOR and the music of Tin Pan Alley for many years. But the rising importance of young people as an audience changed that. Intelligent PDs and MDs have long since learned to keep an eye on demographic trends, that is, what age groups are buying what products. It was because many MOR stations of the 1950s misjudged the potential impact of the young listener that Top-40 was able to take hold. Similarly, a few years later, Top-40 would misjudge the young audience, which was now college-aged. The result was another new format, Album-Oriented Rock (AOR), and it catered exclusively to the young people who by now found Top-40 too predictable. Album Rock, which in its early days was called Progressive Rock, fostered an outrageous image and played songs that Top-40 ignored.

Since many books about radio formats, among them Focal Press's *The Radio Station* by Michael Keith and Joseph Krause, describe what AOR tries to do, let's look at how this new format affected the role of the music director. As we have seen with early Top-40, some stations had a rigid playlist (which would become even more restrictive as a reaction to the payola scandal of 1960). Other stations took a few more chances on new songs, but just by the very fact that Top-40 only played a small number of songs in the first place, there wasn't a lot of experimentation possible. Also, the album as a configuration hadn't really established itself. Top-40 singers did in fact record albums, but more often than not, the album was just a vehicle for the one hit song (the single) that artist had. Singles were what teens bought, and album sales lagged behind. Most pop music formats of that time had become like Top-40 in concentrating their airplay mainly on the hit single. Even formats not aimed at teens had found that the audience preferred the songs they knew. They were wiling to listen to something new, but they really wanted to hear their favorites. It was very unusual for most stations to stress album tracks.

All this changed with the arrival of the so-called British Invasion. While formats such as Country and Black would not immediately feel the effect the way Top-40 did, the mid-1960s definitely altered the expectation young people had about music. Suddenly, the Top-40 charts were dominated by such British groups as the Beatles, the Rolling Stones, the Animals, and others. These groups did much more than put out a hit single. They had a lot of good material, and some of it was on their album, thereby making the album something worth buying after all. As American popular culture was being influenced by British fads and fashions, gradually the album as a creative resource emerged, complete with interesting cover art and liner notes that expressed a group's philosophy (album liner notes had previously been a biography of the artist or some fan of that artist writing about how great the artist's music was).

Top-40 was placed in a difficult position. As a format, it basically played the hits and had won the teens over by doing so, but suddenly, the big groups had more than hit singles to offer. Some stations jumped on the British Invasion bandwagon and played large amounts of British music (Top-40 giant WABC called itself "WA-Beatle-C" to let fans know who played the most Beatles songs), but that still didn't solve the problem. Now, even some American groups were recording albums. Should Top-40 play album tracks from the hit groups or not? By definition, Top-40 was designed to be like a jukebox, a comfortable place where fans knew they could hear the hits over and over. Albums had not been part of the plan.

As PDs and MDs agonized over the newly emerging popularity of albums, social conditions were also changing. Much has been written about the impact of psychedelic drugs and the effect of the Vietnam War on young people of the 1960s. The music was now reflecting a growing unrest and dissatisfaction with the so-called establishment. This was nothing new: popular music had long had a history of being safe and romantic, but there were always performers and genres which broke away and said something substantial. The music scene was showing the influence of folk music, and songs with lyrics that protested war or spoke out against racism were being heard. Top-40, however, wasn't sure these songs fit. Early Top-40 had been about let's party, let's dance, let's shock our folks. Mid-60s music too had some elements of this, but now a different sound was popular, especially with the college students.

There has always been debate among trivia fans as to who the first official Album Rock DJ was. Many people think it was Scott Muni, then a Top-40 DJ in New York, who went on to do Album Rock for over 25 years. In 1966, he and two other Top-40 DJs, Murray the K and Bill "Rosko" Mercer, created a format known as Progressive Rock at WOR-FM in New York City. The noble experiment ultimately failed, but it showed the possibilities of playing album tracks. Meanwhile, around the same time, a West Coast DJ named Larry Miller had a plan: he was doing overnights at KMPX in San Francisco, a station with poor ratings, and he decided a change would do everyone some good. By that time, San Francisco had a thriving rock scene, with numerous local bands, none of which got any Top-40 airplay. Miller began playing these groups on his show. What was significant about both WOR-FM and KMPX was that for the first time, young people were given a reason to choose FM. While FM technology had existed for years, most FMs in the early 1960s were mainly educational or classical. It was AM which played popular music; FM was regarded as a curiosity. But that too changed with the rise of Album Rock.

Music was changing in other ways after the British Invasion began in 1964. Hit songs gradually became longer; in rock's early days, the typical hit was seldom more than 3 minutes long. But as more and more album-oriented groups became popular, record companies who tried at first to edit their songs down to a short enough form that Top-40 could use found that many people preferred the longer version. As the controversy over issues such as segregation and the Vietnam War increased, singer/songwriters began addressing these subjects in their music. Songs with thought-provoking lyrics, such as Simon & Garfunkel's "Sounds of Silence," began to appear on the Top-40 charts. The Beatles too went far beyond the typical pop love song genre. As music became more complex, both lyrically and production-wise (the new album-oriented artists of the mid-60s often made use of unusual special effects to make their songs more memorable), Top-40 PDs and MDs had to listen more carefully. They had to decide if a song fit their station's total sound, but they also now had to be careful about songs with possible drug lyrics. The so-called psychedelic influence was strongly present in many of the album groups, and while college kids might have found all this suitably outrageous, conservative AM advertisers might be offended.

FM radio was free to champion the outrageous and the controversial, since it did not yet have many advertisers. The young people who had once loved Top-40 now saw it as stagnant; Progressive Rock was the new hip music. While Top-40 (and

AM) remained popular, now young adults had a choice. Larry Miller's foray into Progressive led KMPX to adopt the format full time. San Francisco, home of another FM innovator, Tom Donahue, became a hub for Progressive Rock, along with cities like New York and Boston.

The early days of most formats are marked by a lack of rules and willingness to experiment. Album Rock was no exception. The format's first version was done in a free-form style; that is, the announcers (they did not think of themselves as DJs) played anything they felt was appropriate. When I interviewed several of them, I understood more clearly what they had tried to accomplish. Critics of the format accused it of being self-indulgent. Some announcers did in fact seem to have an elitist attitude, believing that passives, those supporters of Top-40, lacked the intelligence to appreciate good music. But some of Album Rock's pioneers truly believed they were striking a blow against safe, conservative radio. They saw their role as educational, but they also wanted people to have the opportunity to hear the new rock music for themselves, without the restrictions of a tightly playlisted station. In free-form, it was always an adventure. Announcers would try to set a mood or develop a certain theme. Unlike today, where stations just play the hit songs or the hit artists, Progressive Rock often featured sets of music revolving around a specific subject, such as a group of antiwar songs, or a group of songs about the environment. Not only would rock music be played, but also jazz, ragas, or whatever else the announcer felt would work; even poetry readings were not uncommon.

As you might expect, soon there were two schools of thought about the right way to do Progressive Rock. One group, the purists, believed that the announcer only should select the music, and those people who didn't like it could go back to Top-40. But another group was more pragmatic: while many college stations had switched over from Top-40 to free-form, some professional FM station managers realized that without good ratings, their station would not make enough money to attract advertisers. The best way to get ratings was to create a station that the passives could enjoy, while still maintaining the outrageous, nonconformist image, and playing the newest music to keep the actives happy. The purists didn't want to play any mass-appeal music; for them, Progressive Rock meant a rejection of the Top-40 methodology. If an album artist had a hit single, that song would not be played. Yet, in order to give the average person a reason to sit through all the unfamiliar songs, some PDs felt it might not be such a bad idea to play a few of those rock hit singles. The debate raged on throughout the 1960s, as Progressive Rock and FM radio continued to grow in popularity.

Pete Fornatele, who became an announcer at successful Album Rock station WNEW-FM in New York, discusses this debate about the format's true purpose in his book *Radio in the Television Age*. At first, he notes, it didn't matter how a station sounded. As with the early days of radio itself, the early days of Progressive Rock were so exciting to its fans that they overlooked the format's flaws. But economics finally won. "Initially, the stations [that did FM Progressive] drew ads from concert promoters, motorcycle shops, 'head shops,' and sandal makers; the only national advertising came from record companies. But as audiences grew, and as sales of FM receivers flourished, more advertisers came on board: manufacturers of musical instruments and stereo equipment. Eventually, airlines and beer companies joined." While a certain degree of outrageousness still survived, the format eventually became more corporate and more polished. The announcers no longer picked their own music, and although Progressive Rock stations still played a wider variety of music than Top-40, they didn't experiment with as many unusual-sounding groups. They no longer played ragas or read poetry, and if a rock group had a hit single, it definitely was played. By the mid-1970s, it was rare to hear anything that resembled free-form. There were a few notable exceptions, such as WHFS in Bethesda, Maryland, and a few respected college stations, but even top-rated WMMS-FM in Cleveland took some of the power away from the announcers and instituted a few format restrictions, among them that the PD and the MD would decide which new records went into the studio (the announcers could, and did, offer their suggestions, but the PD had the final say).

If early Album Rock was free-form, then why did it need a music director? The answer is an interesting one: the role of the MD in Progressive Rock was quite different from what we expect today. Tim Powell was one of the announcers at pioneering KMPX in San Francisco, and he not only saw first hand the format's development; he also saw the different roles at the station become more clearly defined.

> David Kane was the first music director I ever worked with. [Back then in 1968], releases were different between countries. Usually, an important record by a British group would come out first in England; and while it wasn't as common by 1968, there were differences in the cuts on certain albums: there might be an extra cut or two on the British version, something previously unreleased. David Kane was our major source of these English imports. We were in competition with KSAN at the time, [so] there was a . . . need for us to have all the British material ASAP, because Tom Donahue of KSAN was so plugged into the English rock scene. It was a curious time . . . [we] followed every member change in the most obscure groups in England. David Kane helped with this process, plus he made us familiar with a group that wasn't really core back then, The Who. Actually, at KMPX the title of 'music director' was sort of a misnomer, since each disc jockey was the program director or music director of his or her own show. [When I became] KMPX's music director, I too kept track of all the new releases, but by then, the release pattern between the U.S. and England had stabilized, and having a contact in England [who could get you the releases first] was no longer of prime importance, since both releases were the same. By that time, we had accumulated a large number of tapes, which had been given to KMPX by the groups or the producers. It was my job to keep track of these tapes and make sure they were put back [in the right category]. I was also in charge of [talking with] record promoters. I can't stress enough that [in those early days] we were working in a vacuum. The record promoters would deliver the material, but many of them had no idea what we were doing. They were often surprised to find that it was our airplay that sold their albums. In time, they hired specialists to deal with the FM stations.

While Tim Powell worked in Album Rock's free-form years, I was a music director during those transitional years when Progressive Rock was evolving into a more mass-appeal format. My recollection of being a music director in the early 1970s was that it involved disseminating a lot of information to the air staff. I would read the trades, as well as music magazines like *Rolling Stone*, and put 3 x 5 cards on the album jacket, giving pertinent facts about a new group. Of course, many of the announcers at WMMS-Fm already knew a great deal about every artist we played; for them, Progressive Rock was almost a way of life. But other announcers were overwhelmed by all the new releases, which I would put in their bin daily so that they could listen and then offer their opinion about whether the album deserved to be played. For them, having a PD and an MD meant we could take care of the lion's share of the new music listening and there was one less thing for them to worry about.

Another function I served as music director was as the resident resource for Canadian music. I had built a reputation at previous stations for playing good Canadian bands; when I launched the career of Rush, suddenly, every manager of every Canadian band would send me their new releases. I didn't discover any other Rushes, but I made a lot of new friends in Canada. As David Kane had done with The Who at KMPX, I found I could call the announcers' attention to groups they otherwise might have overlooked. While I also spent a lot of time filing records back into the music library, the job of music director at WMMS-FM had considerable variety and was usually fun. But it was not a position with much authority, although there was frequent opportunity to influence the station's music selection.

One other perspective on the role of music director in Progressive Rock radio comes from a man well-versed in the format's history, Mike Harrison. It was he, while an editor at the music industry's weekly newspaper, *Radio & Records*, who renamed the format Album-Oriented Rock (AOR). He did so because by the early 1970s, "progressive" no longer truly explained the format. It had grown to a point where it sold millions of records and had great influence on the careers of many artists, yet it still had an image of "hippie radio." To help the format sound more professional to the advertising community, as well as to reflect its evolution and growing popularity, it needed a name change. Harrison began referring to the format as AOR, and the new name took hold. With his extensive background in both Progressive Rock and AOR, Harrison recalls what the first music directors did. "The record promoters talked to each announcer individually [because we picked our own music]. We got taken out to lunch a lot. Since each of us picked the music for our own shows, we all got a copy of every record. The music director often received all the records and made sure we got our copies. Music directing back then was considered as an entry-level position: you then moved up to being a DJ."

When I talk about the career of music directing, students often ask me if things are better now; that is, do music directors have more authority? I will discuss that question in more detail in an upcoming chapter, but suffice it to say there is no simple answer. Some stations still use the MD as a file clerk, and he or she just receives the new releases and hands them over to the PD. At other stations, the MD helps to decide what is added. At others, he or she actually has the final say. But no matter how much or how little authority the MD has, the job has some excellent fringe benefits. It's a great place to learn about how a radio station is run. You often get to meet celebrities (or groups who will someday be celebrities), and you get to listen to the new music first. In the early days, in fact, you even got to pick out your own music. As Tim Powell mentioned, the record companies still didn't know what to make of Album Rock in its infancy. Since these stations seemed to play such a strange variety of music, the companies had something called "Radio Day." On that one day, PDs and MDs from college and professional Album stations could go to the local companies and, within reason, help themselves. Tim Powell recalls, "Back then, there wasn't the staffing in promotion that there is today. In the 60s, record companies still used distributors to merchandise and sell their product. [Once] I was invited to visit one of the local distributors to take whatever KMPX needed. I was literally walking through [a warehouse with] shelf after shelf of albums, all different labels too." Today, the larger record companies tend to have their own branch operation. For example, Warner-Elektra Atlantic (WEA) will have a branch in each major city (in addition to the home office in New York). Some of these branches may distribute a smaller label that they own, but, in general, the companies themselves promote and publicize their records. Thanks to the success of Album radio, record companies soon added promoters, who knew a lot about the format and promoted it exclusively. (Country record companies had long had such specialists for Country stations, and there were also promoters whose speciality was Black radio.) But picture, if you will, those new music directors back in Album Rock's early days, going to a typical distributor (who might carry as many as 70 labels) and basically being told to take whatever they wanted . . . Those were the good old days!

The success of Album Rock brought about a new phenomenon: there were now numerous groups, Rush among them, who had top-selling albums with no airplay from Top-40 radio. But Top-40 radio was far from dead. In fact, the format had experienced a resurgence. With many people still wanting hits, with FM still a novelty in many cities, AM Top-40 did what it had always done with any fad or trend: it adapted and survived. By the late 1960s, it was no longer an issue as to whether Top-40 should play hits by AOR groups. Top-40 listeners were song-oriented anyway, and they didn't care if the song came from Country, Black, or Album radio, as long as it was a hit that sounded good on the radio. Top-40 was more than willing to be flexible and adjust to the new style. When in 1968 Richard Harris came out with "MacArthur Park," Top-40 stations didn't try to edit it. They played it in its entirety, although it was over 7 minutes long; most did the same with another 7-minutes-plus song, "Hey Jude" by the Beatles. The pop charts reflected a new diversity that kept Top-40 fresh: hits from Album Rock groups like the Doors, Motown soul groups like the Supremes, a few Country artists, an MOR artist or two (Frank Sinatra did a duet with his daughter Nancy and it was a big hit), and the ever-increasing string of hits by such British rock groups as the Rolling Stones and the Beatles. Top-40 was interesting again, and AM was still very healthy.

One final word should be said about the impact of Album radio: as a result of its success, it provided a number of college PDs and MDs with jobs in the music industry. The record companies who needed specialists to promote Album Rock often found them at college radio stations. To this day, I can point out many record company executives, as well as numerous radio station GMs and PDs, whose first introduction to media was the work they did as a music director at their college station.

I had mentioned earlier in this chapter that it was not only Top-40 that underwent changes during the late 1960s and early 70s. Black radio would evolve into what we know today as Urban, incorporating popular music with a dance beat into a mix that could also have Soul or R & B, and, at some stations, most notably the innovative WBLS in New York, perhaps even some jazz. Programmed by Frankie Crocker and music directed by Wanda Ramos, WBLS achieved great popularity during the 1970s. It was in some ways a black version of Album radio, because Crocker and Ramos didn't restrict the station to just 40 records the way traditional Top-40 stations might. WBLS was another in the increasing number of important FM stations. Like an Album Rocker, the station broke new artists and created hit records. It also succeeded in attracting a large number of white listeners. Throughout the 1960s, Black stations were usually relegated to poor signals on the AM band, often run by owners who didn't have much money to do promotions or contests, yet, the music carried them, and many, like the legendary WDIA in Memphis, were very influential in what records would cross over from the Black charts to the Top-40 audience. The success of stations like WDAS-FM in Philadelphia and WBLS in New York showed that Black radio could indeed capture a large audience if given a good signal and a promotion budget.

Gradually, the 1970s saw music stations of all formats move over to FM. Today, there are still some successful Black stations on Am, but the younger audience remains on FM, and Urban radio is extremely popular. (The difference between Black and Urban is frequently one of semantics. In the format's early days on FM, it took the new name in an attempt to combat what some station managers saw as a racist attitude from the advertising agencies. These agencies had a number of stereotypes that prevented certain formats from being bought. For example, Country listeners were supposedly hicks who drove trucks; black listeners were allegedly too poor to be able to purchase much. Hoping to convince agencies that the new Black radio was smooth, polished, and definitely upscale, some stations presented it as Urban, or music that any person, black, white, or Hispanic, who is a city dweller would love. Some Urban stations are really just playing Black music only; others are almost Top-40, leaning heavily toward dance music, but playing any song with a beat, whether by a black artist or not.)

The success of Urban and Black radio stations meant more opportunities for PDs and MD to pick the next generation of hist. Obviously, the more formats that operate successfully, the more different types of music get exposure. From only one basic format, MOR, evolved Top-40. When Top-40 became stagnant, Album Rock emerged. Black radio, which had been loved by young people of all colors since its inception, found it could survive both in its traditional form (once called Soul or R & B) and in its new Urban form. Today, a good music director is one who is familiar with all the major genres (and there are others we haven't gotten to yet), because a hit can come from almost any format and cross over to Top-40, which is today called, CHR, but which still plays the biggest hits.

Other books have discussed in great detail how AM lost its leadership and how music ended up largely on FM. Since this book is about music directing, I won't get into that history much, but it is worth noting that new formats continue to evolve and old ones change as the demographics of the country shifted. The teens who ran home to watch "American Bandstand" in 1958 are now in their forties as this book goes to press. Few of these so-called baby boomers like hard rock anymore, but unlike previous generations, they still enjoy pop music and they still have favorite songs. Some even attend rock concerts, since a number of rock stars are baby boomers too and are still performing. MOR has splintered into Adult Contemporary (AC), a format that plays some current music, some Oldies, but no hard rock; Adult Contemporary used to be thought of as an Oldies format. Today, many ACs play new songs by artists who are especially popular with 25- to 44-year-old adults. Some ACs are almost like CHR stations, except for a lack of teen music. They have hot rotations for the biggest hits, making sure these songs repeat frequently enough so that people just tuning in can hear them. The job of music director at AC stations is no longer a clerical function. Since many AC stations add new songs, report to the trades, and keep their listeners up to date on trends that affect their lives, music directors at ACs have an important job. Some MDs have a difficult time with that job, however, because their own personal taste in music is too young for the audience. Today, Ac has evolved into a format with its own strengths. Large numbers of adults like it because it plays the hits from the past as well as those from the present. It is not unusual for some Ac listeners to share their time-spent-listening to CHR radio. In fact, radio listeners who grew up with Top-40 (CHR) are still song-oriented and will tune around until they hear a song they like, a behavior once associated only with teenagers. AC music directors must keep up with the important adult pop groups, some of whom can be seen on VH-1, a television music channel that emerged when it became obvious that while young people could watch music videos on MTV, adults had nowhere to see their favorite artists. VH-1 has filled that gap and is very successful.

While a large part of this book is devoted to mass-appeal formats such as Top-40 (CHR) and Album Rock, it would be wrong to ignore another major format, Country. As mentioned earlier, Country radio too has seen its share of changes over the past several decades. Where once there were only so-called Country & Western or Traditional Country stations, today Country radio attracts a wide audience in such forms as Modern and Contemporary Country. About the only area where the format has never succeeded is East Coast markets such as Boston and New York City. (Interestingly, in smaller eastern cities, such as Portland, Maine, or Dover, New Hampshire, Country gets huge ratings.)

Country was one of the earliest formats, although its success for many years was mainly in the deep South. While there are a number of Country stations that can claim to be legends (many of which are still successful on AM), one of the best known is WSM in Nashville. For trivia fans, the letters WSM stand for "We Shield Millions," the slogan of the life insurance company that first owned the station. In the early days of Country, the format was sometimes referred to pejoratively as "hillbilly music," but eventually, it became known as Country. WSM quickly became a leader in giving new artists much needed exposure. Country stations from the beginning had opened their studios to local pickers and fiddlers. Some went on to great success; most did not, but the audience loved them anyway. But WSM turned artist exposure into an art form when it began broadcasting "the Grand Ole Opry" in 1925. The show was named, legend has it, by one of WSM's announcers, George Hay, alias "the Solemn Old Judge." Back in radio's early days, stations often tried to present cultural programming, even if it didn't really fit the rest of their format. After an opera performance concluded, Hay ad-libbed, "You have just listened to Grand Opera. Now, we will present Grand Ole Opry." The name stuck, and the show,

STEREO COUNTRY

98 FM KCQ MUSIC PLAYLIST AUGUST 21-AUGUST 27, 1990

LW	TW	TITLE	ARTIST	
3	1	WANTED	ALAN JACKSON	ARISTA
5	2	DON'T GO OUT	TANYA TUCKER/T GRAHAM BROWN	CAPITOL
6	3	I MEANT EVERY WORD HE SAID	RICKY VAN SHELTON	CBS
4	4	NOTHING'S NEWS	CLINT BLACK	RCA
7	5	JUKEBOX IN MY MIND	ALABAMA	RCA
9	6	I COULD BE PERSUADED	BELLAMY BROTHERS	MCA
8	7	I FELL IN LOVE	CARLENE CARTER	WB
12	8	14 MINUTES OLD	DOUG STONE	EPIC
17	9	HOLDING A GOOD HAND	LEE GREENWOOD	CAPITOL
13	10	SOMETHING OF A DREAMER	MARY CHAPIN CARPENTER	CBS
1	11	NEXT TO YOU	SHENANDOAH	CBS
14	12	BATTLE HYMN OF LOVE	KATHY MATTEA/TIM O'BRIEN	MERCURY
15	13	WHEN A TEAR BECOMES A ROSE	KEITH WHITLEY/LORRIE MORGAN	RCA
16	14	MY PAST IS PRESENT	RODNEY CROWELL	CBS
20	15	FRIENDS IN LOW PLACES	GARTH BROOKS	CAPITOL
18	16	TOO COLD AT HOME	MARK CHESTNUTT	MCA
19	17	LIE MYSELF TO SLEEP	SHELBY LYNNE	CBS
2	18	I'M GONNA BE SOMEBODY	TRAVIS TRITT	WB
21	19	STORY OF LOVE	DESERT ROSE BAND	MCA
22	20	HONKY TONK BLUES	PIRATES OF THE MISSISSIPPI	CAPITOL
24	21	BORN TO BE BLUE	THE JUDDS	RCA
10	22	WRONG	WAYLON JENNINGS	CBS
26	23	DRINKING CHAMPAGNE	GEORGE STRAIT	MCA
27	24	PRECIOUS THING	STEVE WARINER	MCA
23	25	SMALL SMALL WORLD	STATLER BROTHERS	MERCURY
29	26	LOVE IS STRANGE	KENNY ROGERS/DOLLY PARTON	REPRISE
33	27	YOU LIE	REBA MCENTIRE	MCA
31	28	MY HEART IS SET ON YOU	LIONEL CARTWRIGHT	MCA
30	29	NOTHING'S GONNA BOTHER ME	FORESTER SISTERS	WB
34	30	HOME	JOE DIFFIE	EPIC
35	31	LONELY OUT TONIGHT	EDDIE RABBITT	CAPITOL
28	32	BOOGIE AND BEETHOVEN	THE GATLINS	CAPITOL
ADD	33	FOOL SUCH AS I	BAILLIE AND THE BOYS	RCA
ADD	34	DANCE IN CIRCLES	TIM RYAN	EPIC
ADD	35	YOU REALLY HAD ME GOIN'	HOLLY DUNN	WB
EXTRA		THE WORK SONG	CORBIN AND HANNER	MERCURY

UPCOMING CONCERTS

SEPTEMBER	8	DA'YOOPERS	SAGINAW COUNTY FAIR
SEPTEMBER	10	SAWYER BROWN	SAGINAW COUNTY FAIR
SEPTEMBER	11	RONNIE MCDOWELL	SAGINAW COUNTY FAIR
SEPTEMBER	15	REBA MCENTIRE/RICKY SKAGGS	THE PALACE OF AUBURN HILLS

▶ *Figure 2 Example of a Country playlist. WKCQ in Saginaw, Michigan, reports to several trades. This is a typical weekly survey, which is also given out to listeners at station events. Notice that some music directors list what label the song is on as a courtesy to the record companies. (Courtesy of MacDonald Broadcasting, Saginaw.)*

which started in a small studio at the station, moved on to its own venue and has been the launching point for a large number of Country performers for over 60 years.

As with MOR, early Country stations left music selection in the hands of the announcers. Some of them became powerful (as we saw with certain Top-40 DJs): George Hay of WSM even had a say in which performers would be on the Opry. Country artists were known for their willingness to tour and perform, even in the smallest town, and it was a combination of radio and jukebox play, along with live performance, that helped them to achieve success.

As a result of the ASCAP strike of 1941, Country artists received airplay on stations that might otherwise have never done so. An entirely new audience in cities up north and in the midwest were thus able to hear this music. While it is true that rock and roll owes a large debt of gratitude to Black music, it also borrowed heavily from a type of Country known as rockabilly, which would influence such early rock stars as Jerry Lee Lewis, Buddy Holly & the Crickets, Bill Haley and the Comets, and Elvis Presley.

Country radio was not as heavily affected by the payola scandal of 1960 as Top-40 was. For one thing, record promotion was aimed at stations with youthful audiences, in the belief that they bought the most records. Perhaps a bit of regional chauvinism was a factor too: most record companies had home offices in New York, and later Los Angeles. What was happening in Nashville probably didn't concern them very much, especially since not a large number of country songs crossed over to Top-40. The companies left Country promotion to their offices in Nashville and spent most of their time trying to get Top-40 to add their new releases. Country was not considered a mass-appeal format; it was stereotyped as something only Southerners would like, and as a result, Country stations were relatively free to decide upon their own music policies, with no pressure from the trades or the record companies. There were Country charts from 1944 on (*Billboard Magazine* first referred to its Country chart as "jukebox folk records"). Today, there are several trades devoted exclusively to Country, as well as sections in *R & R, Billboard,* and *The Gavin Report*. There is even Country music television (the best-known cable network is the Nashville Network, or TNN). Country artists today are very high profile, appearing on a wide variety of TV shows, and still performing in concert in hundreds of cities. Today's Country uses some Top-40 methodology: hot rotations, jingles, fun contests. Some Country stations are still traditional, playing mostly older material aimed at the 45 and over age group. But other Country stations are more youthful in appeal, playing many of the new artists and striving for a polished, modern sound that would attract the 25- to 44-year-old demographic. Although modern Country stations today are usually found on the FM band, giant stations like WSM and WWVA from Wheeling, West Virginia, continue to maintain a loyal following, helped, no doubt, by their image as a Full-Service station with a huge signal that covers 18 states at night. (Stations that do Full-Service are known for in-depths news, sports, and community coverage; more about such stations can be found in my book on Full-Service Radio.)

So, what about Country music directors? To find out, I asked two of Iowa's most experienced Country DJs, since Iowa has long been a hotbed of Country radio activity. Don "Smokey" Smith has many years in Country radio. He began as a performer in the 1930s, and while he and his band were playing live radio concerts in Lawrence, Kansas, his home at the time, he became fascinated by radio. The local station played records (in the 1930s, many stations still preferred live music and avoided records entirely), but it didn't have a lot of them, so it depended on any liver performers who were passing through the area. Although song pluggers were a large part of the live music scene in many cities, Smokey didn't run into many of them during his time as a performer. For one thing, he recalls, song pluggers seemed to concentrate their efforts on the big cities, and he and his band preferred to play the small towns and local radio stations. For another thing, Smokey's band wrote its own material, so it wasn't looking for songs from anybody else. Smokey found he liked the intimacy of doing local radio, and he eventually stopped touring and became a Country DJ. "If you want to know about the music policy at small country stations in the 30s and 40s," he told me, "it was very request-driven. So were our live performances. We used requests to find out which songs we should keep on performing. Radio did that too: the songs people requested got played more often. When I became a DJ in Country radio, that was still true. I was never given a playlist. I just played what I felt were the best Country records, and I went by requests a lot."

It wasn't until the early 1950s, when he was working in Des Moines, that he began to see record promoters. Some, he recalls, were unique characters. Since they had a large territory to cover, they would fill up their cars with records and drive from town to town, stopping at each Country station. One promoter had a school bus which he used as his vehicle of choice. The vast majority of the Country promoters were low-key, very polite, and extremely knowledgeable about the records they brought. Smokey Smith would make up the station's weekly playlist and handle reporting to the trades. During the 1950s, he compiled the list from requests and store research, much like Top-40 had been doing. "It was an honest list. I didn't play anything I didn't truly believe was a good record." And so it was, almost by osmosis, that he found himself music directing. "It happened that way because I worked at a lot of small stations, and not everybody on the staff knew Country music; in fact, some of the stations didn't even play Country all the time. They'd play it in the morning, for example, and then play something different the rest of the day. So I ended up doing all the programming of the Country music. That gave me a lot of freedom to add new records: there was nobody to tell me not to! But I think today's Country stations are over-playlisted. They go too much by the charts. Because of that, a lot of good new records never get a chance." In addition to doing the music at a number of Country stations well into the 1980s, Smokey Smith also did some work as a concert promoter. Thinking back on that experience, he left me with an amusing story. "I'm probably the only promoter who ever *lost* money on Elvis. I was promoting Country shows at a local theater, and I brought Elvis in; this was very early in his career, and nobody had ever heard of him. If only I had been able to bring him in just a few months later, it would have been an entirely different story!"

Another country veteran, Billy Cole, entered the format in the 1960s. Like many men of his age group, he first did radio while in the service. Unlike most of them, however, he was stationed in an unusual place: Greenland. He and his band entertained the troops, and he saw that many of them liked Country music. Soon, he was asked to do a 1-hour Country radio show at the base's station, and so it was that

Country music found a home in Greenland. When Billy returned to the United States, he continued to be a Country DJ. Like smokey Smith, he found himself doing the music, mainly because nobody else knew how to do it. He became one of a select group of overnight DJs who have been entertaining truckers, shift workers, and insomniacs for years on powerful Am stations with clear-channel signals. In some formats, the overnight shift is regarded as unimportant, but that is not the case in Country radio. As a result, overnight DJs have become influential. Many were allowed to create their own special shows and choose their own music. Some booked famous guests, or did telephone talk with listeners who called in from all over the United States and Canada, long before there were toll-free 800 numbers. While most Country stations had established playlists and enforced formatic rules during the daytime hours, the overnight shift somehow was permitted a greater degree of autonomy. Billy Cole worked at WSM during the early 1970s and saw this firsthand. He also saw the special relationship the Country performers had with both radio and the fans. "I remember that it was very common for artists to just drop by the station with their latest record. Del Reeves and Marty Robbins became friends of mine, in fact. There was that kind of closeness at Country stations back then. I'm not saying this to brag about the artists I knew; the fact is that even the big Country stars were friendly with the DJs. You'd pick up the phone one day, and there was Loretta Lynn or Bill Anderson on the line saying they were in town and they wanted to stop by to play their new song or give you their new record. It's so different today. Now, if you want to talk to an artist, you have to go through ten managers. A lot of the personal contact is gone."

Billy worked the overnight shift at 50,000-watt giant WHO in Des Moines for several years, and there too he chose his own music. "Some of the biggest names in Country radio started by doing overnights, and a lot of them decided to stay in that shift because you could build such a loyal following. We were free to be innovative there. For example, I think my overnight show on WHO was the first to do live remotes from a local truck stop every month. Maybe you think nobody would show up at a truck stop at three in the morning, but we always had big crowds; and we saw just as many fans as truckers. Not only that, but we even had some famous guests, like Johnny Rodriguez, C.W. McCall, and Red Sovine. It wasn't even difficult to get them to appear. All I did was call them up and invite them. You could do that with Country stars."

It is not so common today for announcers to pick their own music, even on the overnight shift. The highly competitive ratings quest has convinced most stations, whatever their format, that it's best to be consistent in all dayparts, even overnights. Some small stations still let certain members of the air staff do their own thing, but, in general, whether in Country or Album Rock, most stations today have a defined and enforced music policy. That is largely the result of the payola scandal of 1960, and even though the hearings took place so many years ago, the scandal had a long-lasting impact on radio programming, as well as on music directing.

5

▼
▼
▼
▼
▼

The Payola Scandal

As we have seen, during the days when formats were emerging, there were no set rules about who selected the music, and this didn't seem to worry anyone. So some of the DJs became powerful and some of the record promoters hung around the station a lot. So what? Some PDs oversaw everything even before there were official rules, but others maintained a hands-off attitude as long as the station got good ratings. Then everything changed, in a way that few people in rock radio had anticipated.

First, a disclaimer: I am saddened every time someone in radio or records becomes involved in payola. It bothers me because such incidents always make headlines and give people the impression that the industry where I work is populated by dopers, hustlers, and thieves. Yes, it is true that some people in the music industry have had (ad still have) drug problems, some of which led them to seek out extra money in illegal ways. It is also true, however, and it doesn't get into print much, that many of the people who once had substance abuse problems are now recovered and clean. It is no longer unusual at conventions to find AA meetings, for example, and I can name you a number of industry executives who are justifiably proud of how they've turned their lives around. Not everyone in my industry is on the take. Not every promoter is dishonest, not every PD or MD takes bribes. But that is what I am often asked when I speak at Career Days and job fairs: how can you stand working in an industry which has such a questionable reputation? While my experience isn't typical (how many other radio people don't smoke, don't drink, don't do drugs, keep a Kosher house, teach Sunday school, and have two master's degrees?), I do know what I've seen. I'm not naive: I have been in rooms where drugs were available. In most cases, I felt uncomfortable and left. I have had record promoters, who didn't know me offer me substances, which I had to explain I never use. But was I ever offered money for playing a record? No, and I don't think I'm the only person who can say that. In over 20 years in radio, I've met and worked with hundreds of PDs and MDs. The vast majority were honest, hard-working people who tried their best to do the right thing. While I did get a lot of free concert tickets and a tour jacket or two, what I mainly got was the opportunity of helping a number of rock groups become popular. Of course, there have been PDs and MDs who took bribes, and some record promoters did bend the rules to get their records played on certain key stations, but the vast majority of the people I know, both in radio and in records, do not deserve to be stereotyped as disreputable.

Unfortunately, the truth is that some of the same temptations that led to payola in the past have never disappeared. Few people in any industry ever intentionally set out to take bribes, but some eventually find reasons to get caught up in easy money, and most rationalize their participation. When a number of DJs were indicted during the payola scandal of 1960, most offered a wide range of excuses: problems with drugs, alcohol abuse, gambling debts. Only one or two admitted that greed played a part. A popular DJ from Cleveland, Joe Finan, at first blamed his indictment on everyone but himself; he said a disgruntled record promoter anxious to draw the investigation away from his company had set him up. But finally, Finan (who also later admitted to an alcohol problem) took some responsibility. "I was seduced," he said in an interview long after the hearings ended. "But I allowed myself to be seduced. It was . . . detestable, and I was part of it." Among the charges leveled at Finan were that he was paid $15,000 in so-called consulting fees by record companies, just for listening to certain records. The agreement was that if he then liked the records, he would give them extra airplay. Supposedly, such fees were innocent: record companies saw them as a way to show appreciation to key disc jockeys. But those who were investigating the music industry in 1960 saw something a bit more sinister at work.

The payola scandal developed gradually. As we have seen earlier, some stations, especially those MOR hybrids who were trying to compete against the newly emerging Top-40 stations of the mid-1950s, had begun having someone other than the DJ select the music (since at the MOR stations, few of the announcers knew much about this rock and roll). Usually, the person chosen to select the music was the station's music librarian, some of whom had established themselves as very knowledgeable about all aspects of music. In fact, this practice went as far back as the 1930s; Al Jarvis, perhaps the first disc jockey, recalls that certain announcers preferred leaving the music selection (and the handling of requests) to someone else who knew more about it. As records became more common, music libraries grew, and the job of the music librarian at MOR stations became more important. By the 1940s, some music librarians had assumed considerable power. In Hartford, which, as you know, was considered an important market by record companies that wanted to test new songs, the most influential station was WTIC. But another station also had a large following, WDRC, where the music librarian was a woman named Bertha Porter. Bertha had an almost encyclopedic knowledge of music: if a listener called to ask about a song, chances are she knew which one it was and where to buy it. Her work in the music library along with her ability to keep the announcers informed about the latest trends helped her to move up in an era when women were kept out of management. For that time, she was given much more authority than the average female music librarian. Her program director and co-worker Charlie Parker recalls that Bertha Porter had a talent for being able to pick out hits. She was so respected at WDRC that, long before playlists and computers, she planned out every announcer's show. "She wrote it all down on a yellow legal pad," Parker told me. "Every day she did this. She would plan out how many male vocals, how many female vocals, how many instrumentals. Nothing got played on WDRC unless Bertha included it in your show. The announcers never picked one record; she did it all for them." Parker also recalls how the big stars of the 1940s were so impressed with her reputation that they would call or visit her to ask her opinion about the hit potential of their latest song; and they took her opinion seriously. Years later, when

WDRC had long since switched from MOR to a very successful Top-40 format, Bertha Porter was still there, in a position that had now been renamed from music librarian to music director, but otherwise, nothing else had changed; she was still picking all the music for every DJ and was still able to predict which songs had hit potential. In spite of all the influence she wielded, there is no evidence that she ever accepted money or gifts for airplay: she had a knack for predicting hits, and she enjoyed doing so. But at other stations, that was not always the scenario.

Not every station gave the job of music selection to the most qualified or the most ethical person, and to further complicate matters, large sums of money were becoming an essential part of radio's effort to promote itself and attract new listeners. The evolution of Top-40 meant big-money contests and expensive prizes at many of the larger stations. These stations felt they had to spend as much money as was necessary to be number one in their market. While this must have been exciting for the listeners, it also created a climate where stations that had never done contests before suddenly had to start giving away money just to remain competitive. Yet, despite all the money that was being thrown around, many announcers, especially in the smaller markets, still made very low salaries. Sensing an opportunity, some record companies stepped in to offer prizes for stations that might not otherwise be able to afford them, as well as offering extra cash incentives to hard-working but underpaid air talents. Of course, nothing was specifically spelled out: record companies which provided the gifts did not demand anything in return, but it was usually assumed that the recipients of the gifts and the money would then show their gratitude with some extra airplay. Most did. As you may recall, it was still not illegal in the 1950s to accept a gift; song pluggers had used this method with band leaders for years and nobody saw anything wrong with it. The interaction of promoter and announcer was regarded as if a waiter had just been given a tip; it was just a means of expressing appreciation for good service, according to those involved. In fact, if it had stayed on a relatively small scale, it might have continued unnoticed.

The 1950s, however, were a time of great social change. For one thing, a generation gap was appearing. In the 1940s, the family members didn't have much conflict about music: MOR was what most people preferred, with a small segment of college rebels opting for jazz. But the 1950s saw teens line up in support of R & B and rock and roll, music which parents found loud and difficult to understand. They also were puzzled (and in some cities, offended) by the gyrations in some of the new dances. A further problem was the paranoia of the times. There was no glasnost in the 1950s, and to be a Communist was to be an enemy. There was great distrust of Russia and what people believed it stood for. Also, these were very conservative times, when segregation still existed in certain cities, and when the mixing of the races, even at a dance, was rare. Women, after having successfully held jobs during World War II, were now expected to give them up, stay home, and be housewives; the vast majority did so. Children born after the war ended, the so-called baby boomers, were expected to be traditional, polite, loyal, and patriotic. But something went wrong: this rock and roll music, with its questionable lyrics and insistent beat, was causing the young to rebel. If all this weren't enough to make the average person wonder what was happening to America, it seemed you couldn't even trust your government. Senator Joseph McCarthy said there were now traitors and Communists in high places. People feared dangerous books, dangerous ideologies, dangerous music. In such a climate of suspicion, it was no surprise that rock music, which was being blamed by the older generation for every problem in society, would become the object of an investigation.

Certain historians writing about the payola scandal of 1960 have suggested that ASCAP, angry at how rock music had caused the decline of Tin Pan alley, tried to destroy rock in the hope that "good music" would then make a comeback. Other writers have said the DJs were just scapegoats, and the real villains were the station owners, none of whom ever got prosecuted because they were rich and connected to certain politicians to whom they gave huge campaign contributions, which is an irony in itself, given what the DJs were accused of having done. (Alan Freed once commented that what was called payola and condemned would be called "lobbying" and would be perfectly acceptable anywhere else.) But while there may indeed have been a certain unfairness in who was and was not indicted, some disc jockeys made it difficult to defend their actions.

Few of us who recall the late 1950s can deny that payola occurred or that it hadn't gotten out of hand in some cities. There was even evidence that certain promoters traveled from city to city giving cash awards to those DJs with the highest ratings. Some promoters threw lavish parties for top DJs; others gave away Caribbean cruises. Payola wasn't even an equal opportunity employer: top black DJs were given smaller payoffs that their white counterparts. But black or white, Top-40 DJs with big followings could receive new clothes, new cars, even new homes from record companies. The only rule at that time was that such gifts had to be reported to the IRS. (Needless to say, few DJs complied.)

The height of wretched excess occurred in May 1959, when the Second Annual Radio Programming Seminar and Pop Music Deejay Convention was held in Miami. It sounded fine on paper: a gathering of DJs to discuss the state of the industry. Unfortunately, not much discussion went on. Although some attendees probably did go there to do something constructive, the majority were treated to an array of prostitutes, unlimited free drinks, numerous expensive gifts, free yacht cruises, and more—all courtesy of the record companies. By the following week, it was a front-page news story, under the headline "Booze, Broads, and Bribes," complete with all the gory details. If bad publicity about the alleged evils of rock and roll had made parents nervous, then a newspaper exposé in the *Miami Herald* about what sort of people these rock DJs were didn't improve their opinion of the music their kids liked so much. Soon, even *Time, Newsweek,* and other magazines were covering payola, and they weren't exactly complimentary about rock and roll. Since many rock songs were published by BMI, the folks at ASCAP may very well have been waiting for the growing controversy to bring about rock's demise. That didn't happen, although in some cities, clergy demanded that teens burn their diabolical rock records and return to God.

By November of 1959, the FCC was saying that any announcer who took payola could cause the station's license to be revoked. DJs took the offensive and blamed the record companies, but the government was ready to blame rock and roll. The congressional investigation began in early 1960 and has been thoroughly documented in numerous other books. After the dust settled, Dick Clark emerged reasonably unscathed, as did several other high-profile personalities. But others were ruined, fired, or ostracized. Among them was Alan Freed. Freed certainly wasn't innocent, but some critics felt he was unfairly singled out and punished more severely than DJs who had committed more serious wrongs. The man who was called by some the Father of Rock and Roll died alone and penniless in January of 1965. In a moving tribute to him, rock critic and former A & R executive Arnold Shaw wrote,

> He was certainly one of [rock's] most vibrant . . . personalities, and brought
> an excitement into disc jockey programming that was little known before him. In
> a sense, he was more a proponent of R&B than Rock & Roll, displaying a
> partiality for black artists that limited his national exposure, and by comparison
> to Dick Clark, restricted sponsorships and revenues . . . If he did not invite, he
> surely did not resist the temptations that came with his power. But in the end, he
> was a victim of the war of the Establishment against the new pop music.

The end result of the payola scandal was that record promotion was restructured, and at the radio level, the job of music director was officially created. Some stations became so afraid that they might be accused of payola if they even talked to a record promoter that they overreacted: record promoters were no longer allowed to see the PD or any of the disc jockeys. All records were left with the front-desk receptionist. At other stations, the management began requiring a copy of the weekly playlist to be approved. In some cases, the general manager approved it, or it was submitted to some other executive in the company for scrutiny each week. Still other stations simply gave the program director the power to supervise and approve all new songs. This process didn't just occur at Top-40. Ironically, it also happened in MOR, where few if any DJs had been involved with payola, since the common wisdom had been the MOR stations didn't have many young listeners, so why bother paying off their DJs. Bob Clayton, with his reputation for honesty intact, was made music director at WHDH in Boston after the payola hearings ended; management evidently felt it was better to be safe than sorry.

For people like Bob Clayton, the job of music director was never a clerical job. Clayton was expected to screen every new record to make sure the lyrics were appropriate, catalogue each record so that there was tangible proof as to what records had been received by WHDH, and then place an official stamp on the approved records. Only those records that had the approval of Bob Clayton could be played; there were to be no surprises unless they were cleared in advance. This degree of control was not usually accorded to music directors. Usually, it was the program director who established a station's music policy, and then the music director implemented it. At some stations even today, it is still done that way.

The one long-term result of the payola scandal of 1960 was that the chain of command at most radio stations became very clearly defined. Where in the past it had varied, with some stations having a PD who picked the music and others leaving it up to the big-name DJs, now many of those DJs had been replaced, and the majority of the pop music stations had strict controls as to what they would and would not play. While it was probably frustrating for DJs who had become accustomed to picking their own songs to suddenly find that power totally taken away from them, chances are that the average passive listener wasn't aware that anything had changed. As long as the hits were being played, the audience was happy.

It would be gratifying to be able to tell you that the new rules got rid of payola forever. That, however, wasn't what happened at all. Since there seem to always be a few opportunists, payola simply went underground for a while, and when all the controversy had died down, certain activities resumed; but this time, it wasn't the disc jockeys who were involved; it was certain PDs.

There were still a few stations where certain trusted DJs kept their autonomy; many of these held down the all-important night shift, when the kids were supposed to be doing their homework but in reality were listening to their favorite station waiting for their favorite song. The DJs who did this shift frequently took requests and dedications; many of the requests were songs that were already on the station's approved playlist and were going to be played anyway, but the average passive probably didn't think about that. A select few of these DJs continued to play certain new songs first; but at most stations, the DJ would at least have to let the PD know before doing so, and the song wouldn't be added to the station's playlist if it didn't get lots of reaction from the audience, as well as meeting the approval of the PD. Those DJs who had a good ear for hits sometimes became the station's music director just to be able to continue having some say, however limited, in what the station played.

Nowhere was payola shunned more vehemently than at the corporate level. ABC (today Capital Cities) owned a chain of stations, among them the now-legendary WABC (which during the 1960s and early 70s had some of the largest audiences in the history of Top-40 radio and was consistently New York's most listened to station). Given how influential WABC was to the success of a record, you might think that the record companies would have willingly done anything to get the station to add a song, but, interestingly enough, the station was above reproach. One reason was certainly the strict controls that ABC's executives maintained over the music policy. But another reason was WABC's program director, Rick Sklar. While some PDs had begun to derive the benefits that the DJs had once enjoyed, there were also PDs who had great integrity. Rick Sklar had the ultimate position of power; as PD at New York's No. 1 station, he had the final say as to what records were added each week. WABC was very slow to add songs; the station didn't try to break unproven music. But once WABC finally did add a record, the record company could be virtually certain of a giant hit. Airplay on WABC sold records; that was a fact. But WABC didn't add many records and they were very careful about what they put on the air. Rick Sklar had taken over at WABC when it wasn't yet a Top-40; it had a long playlist, two 5-minute newscasts an hour, and a heavy sports commitment, plus numerous features left over from the station's MOR past. What Sklar did was transform WABC into not just a teen station, but the ultimate in mass-appeal radio for anyone who liked pop music. In his book *Rocking America* he talked about his programming philosophy.

> Music was the key ingredient of WABC's programming. [If I had] any secret formula, it was in the painstaking work of the selection and exposure of each of the records. To generate the biggest ratings in radio, I used the shortest playlist in the business. Most new songs just did not appeal to all the diverse

groups that made up our target audience, so I refused to play them. Once a song did meet our highly selective criteria, it would be played with increasing or decreasing frequency as its popularity changed from week to week.

The record companies probably resented Rick Sklar's policies at first, but eventually, they became accustomed to them, especially as they saw just how much power WABC had in making a song a hit. WABC made its name by only giving the audience major, bona fide hit records and no filler. To be certain he was playing the right songs, Sklar and his staff would call a rotating number of record stores to find out what was selling well and then compile the data. The biggest sellers that fit WABC's sound were considered for official adds. To make sure the information was reliable, Sklar called a different group of stores each week, just in case record promoters might have encouraged certain retail outlets to say good things about a record. Sometimes it took a while, but Sklar prided himself on obtaining accurate store reports somewhere each week. (By the way, for the cynics among you, at the height of WABC's popularity, when it had more listeners than any station in the entire United States, a record promoter friend of mine told me how Rick Sklar asked for a pair of concert tickets for a member of his family. The promoter, certain he could get in good with Sklar this way, eagerly brought the tickets: Sklar immediately paid him what the tickets cost.)

Rick Sklar had a music director, a research director, and various assistants as WABC grew. But Sklar always had total control over the music; no record, no matter who it was by, got on the air without his permission. Thus, as Cousin Brucie recalls in his own book *My Life in Rock and Roll Radio*, when a new hit called "Palisades Park" by Freddie Cannon came out, and the possibility of a major tie-in with the popular amusement park was likely, along with, perhaps, one of the major promotions that WABC became famous for doing, the record couldn't be played until Sklar was called at home to okay it. Any of the DJs who didn't like the new system were invited to leave. No DJ was allowed to pick the music on WABC, although their input at the station's Tuesday morning music meetings was welcome. (In addition to its successful music policy, WABC became known for some incredible promotions and contests; its "Principal of the Year" award generated so many entries that WABC had to hire a temporary staff of 80 to count all the ballots.) WABC had many success stories, and since several books about the station's meteoric rise have already been written, I won't repeat them. Suffice it to say that Rick Sklar proved a program director/music director could be (a) honest, (b) in touch with the hits, and (c) very successful. As he had planned, New Yorkers came to regard WABC as a friend.

Rick Sklar's insistence on total authority over the music would become the rule at many stations during the 1960s. At ABC, and elsewhere, all the disc jockeys and managers had to sign statements that they had not and would not accept gifts from record promoters. (Some stations were so nervous about even the slightest appearance of payola that having lunch with record promoters was forbidden.)

But, as Rick Sklar and others who relied on store research became aware, new forms of payola still managed to pop up. At the retail level, there was a practice known as *free goods*, where a record company would give a record store free boxes of records to sell at a profit (record stores usually had to pay for what they sold and although they received discounts from the various record labels, they still had to purchase the records). Free goods became a way to motivate a store manager to give a song an artificially high report when a station like WABC called. The store got a free box of records to sell, and the record company got a favorable report to some important stations. Of course, this made the information obtained worthless, but those people who participated in this transaction evidently saw no problem. (That was why Rick Sklar always changed his store list on a regular basis, figuring that it would be too expensive and too difficult to bribe every record store in New York every week.)

Another way to hype a record involved trade ads. Although everyone concerned would deny any correlation, it was sometimes observed that record companies who purchased full-page advertisements in certain trade publications saw their records make big jumps up the charts. Fortunately, position 1 to 15 are difficult to fake, I am told by friends of mine in the record business; but, unfortunately, there was a time when the rumor in the industry was that certain charts were for sale, and if a song suddenly moved up from 89 to 30, look to see how many ads that company bought last week. This made the job of the music director and program director more challenging: if they used the national charts as a guide to see what the big hits were, then were they really being shown the big hits, or the big hypes? In that time before call-out research and auditorium testing (which we will discuss soon), it was often difficult to be sure, and PDs and MDs had to rely on their instincts.

While the vast majority of the PDs and MDs did their jobs honestly and maintained their integrity, they never did make the news. But in the 1970s, another governmental investigation revealed that certain record company executives at CBS and Brunswick Records were guilty of income tax evasion and had also given cash payments to certain stations in exchange for increased airplay, that did make the news. In the mid-1980s, when rumors began flying that so-called *indies* (independent record promoters) wielded enormous power and could single-handedly make or break a hit thanks to the huge sums of cash and huger amounts of drugs they used as incentive, that made the news too, and several friends of mine (who happened to be indies but who also happened to be innocent) lost their jobs, despite the fact that they didn't do drugs and had never paid off anyone.

A more recent scandal involves a practice called *paper adds*, wherein a dishonest record promoter and a dishonest PD work together. Each week, major stations report their adds and playlists to the trades. Certain record companies began giving a bonus to indies (and some local promoters too) if they could get a song added to a key station's playlist. The problem was that some PDs would not really add the song: they would just add it on paper (that is, in their report to the trades) and never play it. The particular record promoter would then get the bonus and split it with the PD. The trouble with paper adds is they give an unfair picture of a record's potential. A record needs airplay (as well as exposure on TV through music videos) in order to achieve popularity. Those PDs who added a song on paper but never played it created a distorted playlist. Many small, nonreporting stations look at what the reporting stations have added and use that as a guide. A record that was allegedly added, though perhaps it didn't deserve to be, might cause some other unsuspecting station to think it's a hit; conversely, a song that has hit potential but doesn't get the airplay might give other stations the impression that it was taken off the air (rather than that it was never really on in the first place) because of negative response. So, in the end, a few PDs (several of whom, according to later testimony, had problems with cocaine addiction) compromised their own station's integrity to make some extra money for themselves.

The trades, especially *Radio & Records* (R & R), which is considered by many to be the most influential trade publication, dealt harshly with the stations they found guilty of paper adds. Such stations were removed as reporters, or *delisted*. While that may seem like a slap on the wrist, remember that those stations chosen as reporters often get the best record service, numerous prizes for contests, interviews with celebrity rock stars, and lots of prestige. Being delisted means an end to much of this attention; while most intelligent record companies try to give good service to every station, many do seem to go out of their say for those stations that are reporters.

It is often written that payola was terrible, and that it has done great damage to the music industry. Extravagant payoffs, these writers say, did nothing more than help a number of bad records to become hits. But Professor R.H. Coase offers a somewhat different perspective.

> To sell music on a large scale, it is necessary that people hear it. Payola is one way of inducing people to play it so that it can be heard. From a business point of view, the ban on payola is therefore simply a restraint on one kind of promotional or advertising expense. Before World War II, it was the music publishers who wished to see payola abolished; their aim was to eliminate one dimension of competition and thereby increase their total profits. After World War II, when opposition to payola came from those segments of the popular music industry which were hurt by the rise of the new music and the associated development of new record companies, the aim of [those who] sought to curb payola seems to have been not so much to secure a general benefit for the industry as to hobble their competitors.

There is some truth in this statement: where a small group of major record companies had dominated sales in the pre-rock era, suddenly, as rock grew in popularity, it gave birth to numerous small record labels—Cameo, Imperial, Gone, Vee-Jay, roulette, and Ember to name a few; and they all had hits. (Record companies in rock's early days could be started on a shoestring. One executive noted that he started his with less than $1000.) Since these small companies lacked the promotion budgets necessary to launch a new artist's career, they did whatever they felt they had to in order to obtain the one form of promotion that was possible for them—radio airplay.

On the one hand, during the payola hearings in 1960, testimony indicated that some stations had a large playlist because it enabled them to find room for extra records that would make the record promoters happy. But, from the earliest days of Top-40, people like Gordon McLendon and consultant Mike Joseph had advocated a very restricted playlist, not so much to avoid payola as to avoid playing any bad records. If Todd Storz's theory about radio being a jukebox was correct, then having a tight playlist would make sure the listeners only heard the biggest hits over and over. Some stations still became successful with long playlists, but usually those stations had no competition. Charlie Parker, the PD at WDRC in Hartford during its Top-40 days in the 1960s recalls that at first he knew little about how to do the format, since the station had previously been MOR. "Our first version of Top-40, we had a playlist of 60 songs, and we just played them in order, from song number 1 through son number 60. Then we'd start again. We didn't have any other rotation than that, and for some reason, it worked at the time. But later, we had to change it and put in categories."

What, then, can we conclude about payola and its effect on music directing? For one thing, we can say that as a result of the payola scandals of 1960, it became important for most stations to have a music director. For another, it also became important for most stations to have a specific music policy and somebody to enforce it. Although certain rock DJs damaged both their own reputations and that of rock and roll radio at that time, the disc jockey profession endured, as did rock music. Radio itself did more than endure: it continued to prosper, and more new formats emerged. With each new format would come new duties for program directors and music directors, and even though payola scandals still recur now and then, good PDs and MDs have learned how to separate hits from hypes. Most have research at their disposal and a thorough understanding of how to do their job. Music directing has evolved from a largely ceremonial and clerical function into an involved and important part of a station's operation.

6

Music Directing Defined

There are few stations today that don't have a music director. Perhaps there was no need for such a person in those pre-rock days when live music ruled and guest musicians played whatever they felt they should. But as the various formats emerged and as ratings became so important, stations felt they could no longer leave anything to chance. Also, at some stations where the DJs still picked their own music, each shift sounded so different that there was no total station sound. In order to maintain consistency, as well as to maintain order after the payola scandal, station management found that having a music director was a necessity.

It would be impossible to generalize about how the first music directors in Top-40 were treated. As we saw earlier, some MDs were just former music librarians with a new title. Many were female and had previously served as secretary/ librarian/ scriptwriter (remember that at MOR stations, announcers were expected to only announce, and many of them read from carefully planned scripts). These females who were now called music directors still did mostly clerical work that often included answering the phone and opening the PD's mail, as well as doing the store research and typing the weekly music list. Male MDs too were given office tasks, often running errands for the PD. But the perceptions and expectations of the two were quite different: male MDs were often groomed to become Assistant PD (and PD later on), while most female MDs stayed in that job and were told they could not advance any further since they hand "only" been the music director. But as we discussed previously, the earliest definitions of music directing allowed for little status and less authority at most stations. There was nothing glamorous about filing records, typing up the list, or ordering replacement copies of songs. Decisions were made by the PD, who would sometimes ask the MD's opinion. But even at its most restrictive, Top-40 and, later, Album Rock music directors found the job a great learning experience, even when the only interesting part was seeing the record promoters who came by. Other than being able to socialize, many MDs found they were expected to bring all the new records to the PD, and nothing more was required from them.

So why did stations even bother to have a music director, if the job had no responsibility? Evidently, at some stations, certain program directors liked having an assistant but didn't want an assistant with any power. Also, sad but true, some stations were concerned about their license being renewed, and if all their department heads were white males, the FCC might object. So, they created an important-looking job title, hired a female or a black, and then proceeded to go on as if the person didn't exist.

But not every station ignored its music director, nor was every MD just a glorified delivery person or receptionist. For every MD, male or female, who did little more than type up the cards, file records, and answer the PD's phone, there were other stations where the MD was respected and listened to. We have already seen, for example, the authority that Bertha Porter had, years before feminists were demanding more responsible jobs for women. While radio can certainly be held up as an industry that for years had all too few female program directors and general managers, that finally began changing in the 1980s, especially as more women moved into radio sales and became successful at it. Traditionally in radio, general managers have come from the sales department. Today, there are more PDs making the transition to upper management, but it is still most common for upper management to have had sales experience.

Whether or not it was a direct result of industry sexism, the fact remains that in the 1960s and 70s, women who worked in radio often became music directors. It was especially common for major market Top-40 stations to have a male PD and a female MD, although this certainly wasn't always the case. One of the best-known women in Top-40 was Rosalie Trombley, of CKLW in Windsor which served the Detroit market. CKLW was one of the stations consulted by Bill Drake; others included KHJ in Los Angeles and WRKO in Boston. Although CKLW was technically a Canadian station, its proximity to Detroit gave it great impact, much to the consternation of Canadian record promoters who wished the station had decided to concentrate on Canada rather than on the United States. Bill Drake had a reputation, deserved or not, for running an extremely tight ship, with very limited playlists. At a time when AM radio still ruled, although FM was beginning to make some inroads, Bill Drake made sure his client stations were smooth, high-energy, with a minimum of talk and a maximum of music; he even made some stations cut back on the number of commercials they ran. He also had the final say on every song, as well as on how the DJs would sound. He had listen-lines installed so that he could monitor any of his client stations at any time and he would call immediately if he heard something he didn't like. Like him or hate him, his stations were very successful.

Rosalie Trombley, by her own admission, had few career aspirations when she first came to CKLW: she was divorced, had kids, and needed a job. CKLW needed a receptionist, and she was hired. It is doubtful back then that she knew about Bill Drake, but she did learn about one of his policies right away: PDs and MDs were not expected to spend large amounts of time with record promoters. Frequently, records were left at the front desk with the receptionist. As this occurred each week, she became friendly with some promoters, and began learning more about their jobs. When the opportunity for filling a music director opening occurred, the station's PD, Ted Atkins, offered her the position. Atkins wasn't looking for a typist: he had found that Trombley had an innate understanding of what made a song a hit. Although she was reluctant to take the job in the beginning, soon she was doing what music directors did at Drake stations, similar to what they also did at stations like WABC in New York. She became responsible for doing the store research. "It took two days to call all the stores," she recalls. "I used to contact over 60 stores and one-stops." A one-stop is a place that used to supply jukeboxes and small record stores; it carried virtually every label, so the small stores didn't have to spend time calling all the record companies to place their orders. Gradually, her duties expanded. Contrary to

Drake's image as a tyrant, several of his PDs have told me that they had considerable autonomy, so long as their stations sounded good and got good ratings. Thus, Rosalie Trombley was one of the music directors who was able to have some input into CKLW's music policy. Ted Atkins had a good ear for hits, and he felt she did as well. While he as the PD had the last word, Trombley recalls that he frequently took her advice on a record. "CKLW reported to several trades, so of course, I looked at their charts. But mostly, I tried to pick music that was right for Detroit. People say that the Drake format was rigid, but that's not how I recall it. Our market was a very big R & B market, for example, and we were definitely able to add the right records. Drake always surrounded himself with very bright people. I learned a lot working with Ted Atkins." Rosalie Trombley remained at CKLW for over 20 years, and during that time helped many records become hits.

Another women who worked her way up to music director and turned it into a career was Marge Bush, who was music director at Top-40 station WIXY in Cleveland for many years. Mrs. Bush (she prefers to be called "Mrs.") had been a secretary at WIXY for a long time before the station changed to Top-40. After it made the switch, her boss and mentor Norman Wain, named her the new MD. Since she had never done it, and since most of her radio experience had been clerical, few people took her seriously. But she quickly grew into the job and became determined to do more than just type the music list and open the PD's mail. It took a while for her to get that credibility. "I never tried to be something I wasn't," she told me. "I was older than some of the people at the station, for one thing, and for another, I didn't want to be 'one of the guys.' What I could do was be honest with the record promoters, and choose the records I believed fit WIXY the best. I saw the local promoters on Monday or Tuesday, usually; plus, since we reported to the trades, we got a lot of phone calls from the national reps. Then, we would have our station music meeting, which was on Tuesday afternoon and was attended by the PD, me, and sometimes the general manager."

Like other music directors, Marge Bush used requests and store reports to determine what records were the most popular. Like Rosalie Trombley, she worked at an AM Top-40 station that was dominant for a long while. When FM and Album Rock overtook AM Top-40 in the mid-1970s, many AMs changed format and left Top-40 (later renamed CHR) usually changing to MOR or Oldies. Today, Rosalie Trombley works at a Toronto AM Oldies station, while Marge Bush is the director of the Ohio School of Broadcasting.

Since the job of the music director was fairly new, compared to that of the program director, it varied from station to station, but then so did the job of PD. The first Top-40 PD was probably Bill Stewart of Todd Storz's Omaha station, KOWH. It was he who set the music policy, and you might be amused to see how it was done back then. Bill Stewart obviously had the same problem that would beset Charlie Parker at WDRC in Hartford (and many other PDs) a few years later. He had a concept, but no concrete or established way of doing it, nor any other stations to which he could compare his version of Top-40. Charlie Parker didn't realize that it might not be a wise plan to play songs in strict ranking order. The top songs would play and the listener would then be stuck listening to over 2 hours of new and marginal music before the end of the list was reached. It may have made sense on paper, but in reality it didn't sound good: even in Top-40's earliest days, people wanted to hear plenty of hits. Bill Stewart did know about rotation, but his first attempt t a format involved playing only *ten* records over and over. Todd Storz felt that this small number reflected the number of actual hits, as well as the typical number of well-known songs on a jukebox. It didn't take both Storz and Bill Stewart long to realize that a radio station couldn't survive playing only ten songs repeatedly. People would get tired of them quickly. So, common sense (by means of trial and error) prevailed, and Stewart added a few more songs to the mix.

As we mentioned earlier, Gordon McLendon at KLIF in Dallas began with 25 records in rotation. A few years later, some stations were using playlists of approximately 30 songs (the surveys I collected from Drake stations refer to the "Boss 30"). As to why the format became known as Top-40 although few stations ever seemed to play 40 records, Chuck Blore, who was McLendon's PD in those early days, recalls, "The 40 idea happened because [the DJs] were on the air for 3- sometimes 4-hours. [Since we] played about thirteen records an hour, we figured ten of them should be hits, two should be Oldies because Gordon liked Glenn Miller, and one had to be a new record . . . And you wouldn't want to repeat the same record in the same show, so we multiplied the ten hit records times a four hour shift, and that's where the expression Top-40 came from." If it seems the math is a little off, since he didn't include the new records or the Glenn Miller Oldies, don't be concerned. The MOR songs obviously didn't survive for long anyway, and perhaps they didn't always play 13 records. But you get the point.

For much of this book, we've looked at the conditions that led to the creation of the music director's job: format radio, payola, etc. As it is impossible to generalize about how music directors used to be treated in the early days, it's equally difficult to make a blanket statement about how they are treated now. Looking back at my own years of music directing, I worked at one station where I had no say in anything, another where I had almost total say, a third that was somewhere in the middle, and a fourth that started out looking rather limited and quickly expanded into a PD job. We will hear from some of today's music directors in the next chapter, but for now, let me just say that even at the stations where MDs mainly file the records and CDs or type the cards, new opportunities do present themselves, and many MDs I know have found they have a great deal of input into the station's music policy.

It might be helpful at this point to give a general job description for music directors. I am well aware that not all MDs in all markets do every single thing I am about to list. But what follows is a fairly complete look at the most common duties and responsibilities of a music director, be it in a small market or a large one. While some small stations can't afford a music director and expect the PD to do the job in addition to all his or her other duties, it's safe to say that at the stations which do employ a music director, these functions are typical.

First, for those who are unfamiliar with radio station hierarchy, the chain of command at the average station is usually this: the owner, who may be there daily, or have no direct involvement, is the chief executive. After the owner, and especially at stations where that person is an absentee, the general manager is next in command. As noted earlier, most GMs got their start in sales, where they were account executives (a nonsexist euphemism for salesmen), then local sales managers, and eventually they were promoted to the GM position. This job usually has considerable authority. Sometimes, the GM is also a part owner, and may have vice president added to his or her title. Years ago, GMs were almost exclusively male; today more women attain this level, just as there are also more women who own stations.

Reporting to the GM is the general sales manager (GSM), whose job is to oversee the sales department and make sure a consistent flow of commercial advertising comes in. While many listeners regard commercials as annoying, those of us in the industry are all too aware that without advertising revenues, the station would go out of business. Many GSMs (and some GMs too, especially in smaller markets) actually go out and call on clients, in addition to supervising the members of the salesforce.

Also reporting to the general manager is the program director. The PD is in charge of the entire programming department and is responsible for the station's on-air sound. PDs hire and train announcers, help t choose the station's format and then implement it, plan the station's contests and promotions (along with a promotions director, if the station has one), oversee any research the station does, and, at the majority of stations, also do an on-air shift themselves. In the past few years, the PD job has become more highly regarded at many stations. Where it used to be only the GM and GSM who made major decisions about the station, today many stations include the PD in that process and regard the position as another management function. (In radio's early days, and, unfortunately, still at certain stations, some PDs were looked upon as glorified DJs, with little power other than scheduling the announcers. Today, many PDs work with budgets, hire and fire within their departments, and make decisions that will affect the entire station.)

At All-News or News Talk stations, the news director is regarded in much the same way as the program director is at music stations. While most music stations do in fact have a news director, the position is less important, obviously, at a station that doesn't have a large news commitment. For that reason, news directors are seen as co-equal to the PD if the station is news-oriented, and subordinate to the PD if the station is music-oriented. In either case, the news director is part of the programming department and still reports to the general manager. The news director is responsible for overseeing the reporters and other members of the station's news team; at small stations, the news director may also be a reporter and do an air-shift reading news, in addition to performing other duties, such as scheduling staff to attend local meetings and interviewing local newsmakers.

Next on the chain of command is the music director. The MD reports to the program director, and, by implication, also reports to the GM (since just about everybody except the owner does). At the majority of stations, the music director also does an air shift. MDs are sometimes seen as department heads (along with chief engineers and production directors), and at such stations, they attend all department head meetings with the GM, to help formulate and discuss station operations. The MD usually supervises the disc jockey staff, making sure they follow the format. At some stations, MDs help the PD schedule the air staff, and they may even help critique announcers. But, again, while there is no ideal job description, the following are the most common duties of today's music director.

1. Keeps in contact with the record promoters, either by phone or in person. Usually, promoters visit the key stations, but at the smaller stations, they tend to do

most of their business over the phone or by way of the fax machine. (Faxing, which became popular in the late 1980s, added a new dimension to the way record promoters could communicate with stations. Many promoters, who are often called *record reps* now—they were once commonly called *promo men*, but since they are no longer always male, the name was changed—send the latest information about the songs they are promoting to important stations via fax, which enables the MD to see the information even at times when the promotion person isn't able to pay a personal visit.)

2. Receives the new records and makes sure the station has enough copies. In years past, what was sent or delivered to the station were 45 rpm singles. Today, record companies by and large have discontinued the 45 and send stations the singles on compact discs. These are supposed to be of better quality and last longer. (At album-oriented stations, the same process has been occurring. While writing this book, I spoke to several major record company branch managers, who predicted that the vinyl album, or LP, will not survive the 1990s. They felt that by decade's end, all radio stations would receive only compact discs.) Record service is an important concern for stations, who want to have the hits at the same time, if not sooner, as their competitors. Some small stations say they don't receive as good or as fast service as the majors. It is often up to the music director to create the channels of communication that lead to improved record service for the station.

3. Changes the music weekly. This means removing any songs from the studio, be they on record or compact disc, that the station has decided to no longer play (such songs are often called *drops*, to differentiate them from new songs the station has decided to begin playing, called *adds*), and then putting into the studio any songs that have been added to the playlist. At most stations, the air staff is only allowed to play what is in the studio, approved for airplay, and only songs that are on the station's playlist. At some stations, the music is not played directly from the record or CD; it is recorded onto what looks like a small version of an eight-track tape, called a *cart*, and the carts are played instead. This practice is most common at stations that either don't have CD equipment or play a limited number of songs over and over. Often, it is part of the music director's job to go into the station's production studio and record the week's new adds onto a cart.

4. Reads the trades and follows the national progress of the hits. While not all formats look at new hits (Oldies stations are more concerned with the hits of the past, for example), the majority of music stations do play some amount of current music, and the charts found in the trades can be a useful guide as to what new songs are popular. The music director knows the format of his or her station and is able to follow the new songs that would be appropriate for the station.

5. Does local research to find out what is selling. As we have seen, some of the best PDs and MDs from Top-40's past (as well as from other formats) have used store research to keep an eye on what songs are getting good local reaction. Obviously, for stations that are hit-oriented, playing the most popular songs is the intent, and asking the stores for information about what people are buying is one way to find out what is popular. Store research is not infallible, however. Even in markets where the reports are totally honest, passives don't always rush to the store to buy music, even if they love a record. So, stations have had to develop other ways to

Michel'le

91/6 UP54 Same19 Down1

R&R #40–36 BB LP #62-68 BB Hot 100 #43*-40*

12" Sales #16*-10*

*Key Adds Include: KDWB, WPLJ, WSSX, WYYS, KTXY, KQIZ

*12" Sales Reach Top 10 Nationwide

*7th Most Active Record R&R

*All Extrax Must Be Converted To Debuts!

19 Sames Is Uncalled For!

*Please Address All Lateral And Slow Moves!

*Use Tour With M.C. Hammer To Solidify Airplay!

*Average Move +2

*10 Day Single Is Over 44,000! LP Sales Over 563,000!

Michel'le...On The Urban Side

*"Nicety" 66/12. +12 Conversion Factor
With 16 Heavy

*Have Four Stations Reporting This Record Hot!

*WBLS In NY Comes In! Huge Add!

*Please Work With Urban Rep & Push Them
To Close This Record Out & Get Conversions!

Track Goes #30-23*-Great Move!

▶ ***Figure 3a*** *Record companies have promotion staffs whose job is to make radio stations aware of the new releases. These are examples of typical fact sheets from Atco Records, giving the promotion staff the necessary information to persuade the music director to add a new record. (The numbers refer to how many stations added it that week, and its chart position in the trades.)*

BOSTON
Rod Stevens

A	43%		2W	LW	TW
	WXKS, Boston 2.0	1	27	23	20
	WAAF, Boston .5				
	WZOU, Boston 2.0		24	21	19
	WPRO, Providence 1.5		35	31	25*
	CKOI, Montreal				
	WERZ, Exeter	2			
	WFLY, Albany 1.0				
	WRCK, Utica .5		on	on	on
	WSPK, Poughkpse 1.0				==
	WTIC, Hartford 1.5		30	22	19
	WKCI, N Haven 1.5		30	26	22
	WKPE, Cape Cod	3			
	WWFX, Bangor				
	WTHT, Portland 1.0				
	WWGT, Portland .5		on	on	on
	WXXX, Burlington .5				on
	WGY, Albany 1.0		36	32	28
	*WHMP, Springfield .5	B			
	*WKSS, Hartford 1.5				
	*WFHN, Bedford .5				
	*WIGY, Bath .5				
	WVKZ, Albany .5				

MINNEAPOLIS
Denise George

A	8%		2W	LW	TW
A	KDWB, Mnpls 2.0	1			A
	WLOL, Mnpls 1.5				
	KZIO, Duluth	2			
	WTBX, Duluth .5		==		==
	WDAY, Fargo .5	3			
	KPAT, Sioux Falls				
	KYYY, Bismark				
	KQHT, Grand Forks				
	KFMW, Waterloo .5				
	KQCR, Cedar Rapids .5				
	KLYV, Dubuque				
	*KGLI, Sioux Falls .5	B			
	*KKXL, Grand Forks				

LOS ANGELES

A	63%		2W	LW	TW
	KIIS, L A 2.5	1			
	KPWR, L A (1A) 2.5				
	KQLZ, L A 2.5				
	KGGI, Riverside (1A) 1.5			on	18
	KKLQ, San Diego 1.5		on	on	==
	KKFR, Phoenix (1A) 1.0		==	==	13
	KZZP, Phoenix 1.5		26	24	22
	KOY, Phoenix 1.5	2	25	20	16
	KCAQ, Oxnard 1.0		19	16	13
	KKXX, Bakersfield 1.0		26	21	17
	KROQ, Tucson 1.0		A	30	25
	KQMQ, Honolulu 1.0				
	KIKI, Honolulu 1.0		21	17	14
	KLUC, Las Vegas 1.0		22	22	22
	KHTY, S Barbara .5	3			
	KZOZ, S Luis Obispo		37	31	28
	KSLY, S Luis Obispo		31	25	25
	KYRK, Las Vegas .5	B	12	10	9
	*KEZY, Anaheim 1.0				
	*XHTZ, San Diego 1.0				

▶ ***Figure 3b*** *This provides promotional highlights the reps will use when talking to the music director. Notice how the records are tracked according to individual cities, each of which has a local rep responsible for getting the records played. (Both courtesy of Atco Records and Warner/Elektra/Atlantic, Boston Branch.)*

determine what their audience likes. One commonly used method is music testing. This can be done in several ways—either over the phone, called *call-out* research, or in a large room with between 100 and 300 participants, called *auditorium testing*. In call-out, usually the MD prepares a tape that contains identifiable but short segments of songs to be tested. This is called a *hook tape*, and its purpose is to give respondents a chance to express their opinion about each song. Do they still like it? Are they sick of it? Do they hate it? Is it their favorite? While this type of research too has it's pros and cons (how much can a listener decide based on hearing 15 seconds of a song over the phone, for example?), it is used by many CHR stations and some Country and Urban stations as well. A number of good books about how to do such research are available from the National Association of Broadcasters' bookstore in Washington, D.C., and can be ordered by any station that doesn't know how to set up a research system. In auditorium testing, all the respondents, who have been selected in advance and are qualified to make sure they are the right age and listen to the station in question, are gathered in either a hotel meeting room or some other large conference area, and the hook tapes are played. This enables stations to get more information from a larger group of people than they might by trying to find willing participants during the call-out process. The bottom line is that at stations that have the money to do research projects, the music director often supervises or helps the research company set them up and also helps decide which songs will be tested.

6. Listens to new records and picks the most appropriate ones to bring to the weekly music meeting. Where years ago record labels issued a small number of new songs, today literally hundreds cross the MD's desk each month. Obviously, not all of them will be hits, nor will all of them fit every station's sound. Music directors screen the new releases, seeking out songs that not only have hit potential but sound right for the format. Is a song too harsh or strident for an adult contemporary station, for example? Does it sound too Country or too teen or too whatever else for a particular market? While some CHR stations play a lot of crossover music (that is, songs which originally came from another genre, such as Black or Country or Album Rock), others try to play only what they consider safe and potentially nonoffensive. Similarly, Album stations don't want to play an artist who sounds too mellow or "wimpy"; Country stations avoid songs that sound too much like CHR/pop songs (although if the song ends up being a big hit and it seems as though everybody likes it, the station may eventually add it anyway). In every format, there is some music that just doesn't sound as if it fits in with what the station is doing. For years, Album stations were accused of racism for never playing any black artists (except Jimi Hendrix). The reasoning offered was that it had to do with the sound of the music more than the color of the artist. At a time when most big-selling Black hits were dance-oriented, AOR stations found it difficult to locate songs that had a rock sound to them. Today, more black groups are doing music that fits Album Rock, evidently, because more AOR stations are adding them. We also see this crossover phenomenon in other formats. Adult Contemporary radio seldom used to play anything with a rock sound to it. Today, however, there are several different forms of AC radio, one of which is true to its MOR roots and stays away from rock, the other of which plays any CHR hit as long as it isn't too loud or doesn't have too much teen orientation. These and other format distinctions make the job of the music director even

CHR

3 WKS	2 WKS	LW	TW		
6	3	2	❶	**MADONNA**/Vogue (Sire/WB)	
1	1	1	2	**SINEAD O'CONNOR**/Nothing Compares 2 U (Chrysalis)	
8	5	4	❸	**JANET JACKSON**/Alright (A&M)	
10	7	5	❹	**HEART**/All I Wanna Do Is Make Love To You (Capitol)	
20	14	9	❺	**M.C. HAMMER**/U Can't Touch This (Capitol)	
16	10	8	❻	**WILSON PHILLIPS**/Hold On (SBK)	
9	8	7	❼	**R. STEWART w/R. ISLEY**/This Old Heart... (WB)	
3	2	3	8	**CALLOWAY**/I Wanna Be Rich (Solar/Epic)	
25	20	13	❾	**ROXETTE**/It Must Have Been Love (EMI)	
21	17	14	❿	**LINEAR**/Sending All My Love (Atlantic)	
14	12	11	⓫	**SWEET SENSATION**/Love Child (Atco)	
5	4	6	12	**MICHAEL BOLTON**/How Can We Be Lovers (Columbia)	
24	18	15	⓭	**EXPOSE**/Your Baby Never Looked Good In Blue (Arista)	
13	11	10	14	**AEROSMITH**/What It Takes (Geffen)	
28	23	18	⓯	**PERFECT GENTLEMEN**/Ooh La La (Columbia)	
—	31	22	⓰	**PHIL COLLINS**/Do You Remember (Atlantic)	
38	26	20	⓱	**BELL BIV DEVOE**/Poison (MCA)	
34	25	21	⓲	**JUDE COLE**/Baby It's Tonight (Reprise)	
—	34	23	⓳	**RICHARD MARX**/Children Of The Night (EMI)	
32	28	24	⓴	**GIANT**/I'll See You In My Dreams (A&M)	
18	16	16	21	**ADAM ANT**/Room At The Top (MCA)	
7	6	12	22	**BABYFACE**/Whip Appeal (Solar/Epic)	
2	9	17	23	**JANE CHILD**/Don't Wanna Fall In Love (WB)	
40	35	30	㉔	**AFTER 7**/Ready Or Not (Virgin)	
BREAKER			㉕	**PARTNERS IN KRYME**/Turtle Power (SBK)	
—	—	35	㉖	**TAYLOR DAYNE**/I'll Be Your Shelter (Arista)	
36	32	29	㉗	**BASIA**/Cruising For Bruising (Epic)	
30	27	26	28	**FLEETWOOD MAC**/Save Me (WB)	
BREAKER			㉙	**B-52'S**/Deadbeat Club (Reprise)	
39	36	33	㉚	**ELECTRONIC**/Getting Away With It (Factory/WB)	
4	13	19	31	**LISA STANSFIELD**/All Around The World (Arista)	
—	—	39	㉜	**DEPECHE MODE**/Enjoy The Silence (Sire/Reprise)	
11	19	27	33	**MOTLEY CRUE**/Without You (Elektra)	
12	15	25	34	**SEDUCTION**/Heartbeat (Vendetta/A&M)	
BREAKER			㉟	**LOUIE LOUIE**/Sittin' In The Lap Of Luxury (WTG/Epic)	
19	22	28	36	**DON HENLEY**/The Heart Of The Matter (Geffen)	
15	21	32	37	**LUTHER VANDROSS**/Here And Now (Epic)	
DEBUT ▶			㊳	**BRENT BOURGEOIS**/Dare To Fall In Love (Charisma)	
DEBUT ▶			㊴	**WHISTLE**/Always & Forever (Select)	
DEBUT ▶			㊵	**MICHEL'LE**/Nicety (Ruthless/Atco)	

▶ *Figure 4a   The back page of Radio & Records contains the important charts that music directors look at to see how songs are doing nationally. This CHR chart will be widely read and studied. Record companies strive to get enough adds to qualify for a Breaker, a sure sign the song will become a hit. (Courtesy of Bob Wilson, Publisher, Radio & Records.)*

Playlist for Week Ending Friday August 31, 1990

TW	LW	
(1)	1	Janet Jackson— Come Back (A & M)
(2)	3	Poison— Unskinny Bop (Capitol)
(3)	4	New Kids— Tonite (Columbia)
(4)	5	MC Hammer— Seen Her (Capitol)
5	2	Sweet Sensation— Wishes (Atco)
(6)	9	Jon Bon Jovi— Blaze (Mercury)
(7)	11	Prince— Thieves (WB)
(8)	14	Paul Young— Oh Girl (Columbia)
(9)	10	Wilson Phillips— Release Me (SBK)
(10)	13	Bell Biv Devoe— Do Me (MCA)
(11)	16	Phil Collins— Something Happened (Atlantic)
(12)	17	Slaughter— Fly To The Angels (Chrysalis)
13	8	Keith Sweat— Make You Sweat (Elektra)
(14)	19	After 7— Can't Stop
(15)	20	Stevie V— Dirty Cash (Mercury)
(16)	21	Nelson— Love And Affection (DGC)
(17)	18	Kyper— Tic Tac Toe (Atlantic)
18	6	Mariah Carey— Vision (Columbia)
(19)	22	Alannah Myles— Lover Of Mine (Atlantic)
(20)	23	Gene Loves Jezebel— Jealous (Geffen)
(21)	27	George Michael— Praying for Time (Columbia)
(22)	24	Indecent Obsession— Tell Me (MCA)
(23)	30	Cheap Trick— Can't Stop Falling (Epic)
(24)	28	James Ingram—Don't Have the Heart (WB)
(25)	26	Favorite Angel— Only Women (Columbia)
(26)	34	Concrete Blonde— Joey (IRS)
27	7	Seduction— Could This Be (A & M)
(28)	32	TKA— Give Up ON You (WB)
(29)	36	Breathe— Say A Prayer (WB)
(30)	35	Dino— Romeo (Island)
(31)	33	Tommy Page—The Radio (WB)
(32)	36	Michael Bolton— Georgia (Columbia)
(33)	37	Pebbles— Benefit (MCA)
(34)	38	EN Vogue— Lies (Atlantic)
(35)	EX	Duran Duran— Violence (Capital)
(36)	40	Beats International— Won't Talk (Electra)
(37)	EX	Glenn Medeiros— Still Missing (MCA)
(38)	EX	George La Mond— Look Into (Columbia)
(39)	EX	World Party— Message (Chrysalis)
(40)	EX	David Baerwald— Dance (A & M)

▶ *Figure 4b   Example of a CHR playlist from a small-market station. F101 would report this to several trades. (Courtesy of WFAL, Falmouth, Mass.)*

Figure 4b (continued)

Extras
Depeche Mode— Policy of Truth (WB)
Railway Children— Heart (Virgin)

New Adds
INXS—Suicide Blonde (Atlantic)
Ms Adventures— Undeniable (ATCO)
Janet Jackson— Black Cat (A & M)
Billy Idol— L. A. Woman (Chrysalis)
Deee-Lite— Groove In The Heart (Elektra)

Drops
Aerosmith— Other Side (Geffen)
2 Live Crew— Banned (Atlantic)
Billy Idol— Cradle (Chrysalis)
Snap— The Power (Arista)
London Choir Boys— Don't Love You (Capitol)
Venice— People Laugh (Atlantic)

NOBODY PLAYS MORE MUSIC
July 24, 1990

LW	TW	TITLE/ARTIST	LABEL
1	1	H Rub You The Right Way/Johnny Gill	MOTOWN
4	2	H Vision Of Love/Mariah Carey	COLUMBIA
5	3	When I'm Back On My Feet/M. Bolton	COL.
3	4	Poison/Bell Biv Devoe	MCA
15	5	H Cradle of Love/Billy Idol	
6	6	I'll Be Your Shelter/Taylor Dane	ARISTA
9	7	Girls Nite Out/Tyler Collins	RCA
12	8	H Jerk Out/Time	REPRISE
14	9	H Unskinny Bop/Poison	
2	10	Step By Step/New Kids	COLUMBIA
8	11	U Can't Touch This/MC Hammer	CAPITOL
13	12	Girl I Used To Know/Brother Beyond	EMI
16	13	Come Back To Me/Janet Jackson	
11	14	Possession/Bad English	EPIC
17	15	Tonight/N.K.O.T.B.	
19	16	Stranger to Love/Paul Peterson	
7	17	It Must Have Been Love/Roxette	EMI
21	18	Blaze of Glory/Jon Bon Jovi	
20	19	My Kind of Girl/Babyface	
22	20	The Other Side/Aerosmith	
24	21	Release Me/Wilson Phillips	
25	22	Have You Seen Her/MC Hammer	
23	23	Could This be Love/Seduction	
26	24	Oh Girl/Paul Young	
27	25	If Wishes Came True/Sweet Sensation	
AD	26	Thieves in the Temple/Prince	
	27	Epic/Faith N More	
AD	28	Do Me!/Bell Biv Devoe	

LISTEN FOR THIS HOT NEW MUSIC!!
Love & Emotion/Stevie B.
All The Way/Calloway
Make You Sweat/Keith Sweat
How Bad Do You Want It/Don Henley
26 Thieves in the Temple/Prince
28 Do Me!/Bell Biv Devoe
Only Women Bleed/Favorite Angel
Live Like a King/Brojos
Can't Stop Falling in Love/Cheap Trick

KDWB 101.3 FM

▶ *Figure 4c   Example of major-market CHR playlist. KDWB is regarded as one of the most influential CHRs in the United States. Many small-market stations will look at the playlists of major-market stations to get an idea of what the big hits are. KDWB's playlist is reprinted in Radio & Records, along with other parallels from major markets. (Courtesy of KDWB, Minneapolis.)*

Music Programmed for Your Station Friday, August 24, 1990

Daypart: Morncrew 5am　　　　　　　　Friday, August 24, 1990

Title	Artist	Tempo	Intro	Length	Ref#
Words of Love	Mamas & Papas	MU/C	:12	2;10	924
All in the Game (was #1 for 6 weeks in 1958)	Tommy Edwards	DN/C	:00	2:33	630
We May Never Pass This Way Again	Seals & Crofts	MU/F	:11	4:12	828
Something Stupid (reached #1 in 1967)	Frank, Nancy Sinatra	DN/F	:11	2:30	40
I Keep Forgetting (former lead vocalist of Doobie Brothers)	Michael McDonald	MU/F	:20	3:23	259
Just When I Needed You Most	Randy Van Warmer	DN/F	:19	3:53	255
Hello Dolly (reached #1 in 1964)	Louis Armstrong	UP/F	:11	2:16	831
Don't Go Breakin' My Heart (with Kiki Dee; #1 in 1976)	Elton John	UP/F	:13	4:08	787
Smoke Gets In Your Eyes (reached #1 in 1959)	Platters	DN/C	:05	2:38	LIB.
Blue Tango	Leroy Anderson	MM/F	:00	2:51	160

Total Scheduled music 30min. 34 sec.

▶ *Figure 5 This page shows a typical hour of music programming for the morning show of an Adult Contemporary station aimed at listeners over 35. The computer has not only chosen the songs, but it also lists tempo (MU means medium up-tempo) and length, plus any comments the MD wanted inserted. Many stations use a computer for music selection. (Courtesy of Halper & Associates.)*

more crucial, because even if a song is a hit, if it alienates the audience, what good is it for the station to play it? Program directors, who are often very busy, rely on their music director to pick out the best new records that will enhance the station's air sound.

7. Keeps the record library organized and up to date. Music directors know from experience that many DJs can't spell. Others are in too much of a hurry to properly file back what they played. As a result, especially at AOR stations, it's an ongoing problem keeping things in order and easy for the next person to find. Many stations have a numerical system, in the hope that at least most people can count. As for filing records, most stations use the same system a record store uses: alphabetical by artist. I was taught that when deciding how to file a group, the rule was that if the group's name was *really* the name of somebody in the group, it was filed by that

person's last name. In the group Tom Petty and the Heartbreakers, there really is a person named Tom Petty, and the album is filed under *P* for Petty. On the other hand, in the group Steely Dan, there's nobody by that name in the band. Nor is there a Marshall Tucker in the Marshall Tucker Band, and no, there's nobody named Pink in Pink Floyd. In groups where this occurs, you file under the *first* letter of the group—*S* for Steely, *M* for Marshall, and *P* for Pink. Pretty simple, once you get the hang of it. When filing Simon and Garfunkel, since there really is a Simon, it goes under *S*. When filing The Jeff Healey Band, file under *H*, since there really is a Jeff Healey. But since there is not a Lynyrd Skynyrd in the group (although the group did name themselves after a real person they once knew), you would file their albums the way a record store does, under *L*, and *not* under *S*. This is one of the more frustrating (but amusing if you have a good sense of humor) aspects of music directing, as libraries seem to have a mind of their own about never staying in alphabetical order for long.

8. Types the weekly music list and lets the trades know what was added. As we discussed earlier, some stations are what is called *reporters*, and they have to tell the trade or trades to which they report what their adds and drops were each week. Record companies are very interested in this information and use it to help calculate a song's hit potential. It is usually the music director who is the liaison person at the station, giving that information to the trades as well as to whatever record promoters call to ask. Again, the new popularity of fax machines enters in here, as some stations will fax their report to the trades rather than calling.

9. Compiles and tabulates requests. Not all stations take requests or pay much attention to them, but for formats that regard listener reaction as important, keeping a tally of who asked for what can be useful. Some listeners too are now using the fax machine, sending requests and dedications that way. Other listeners just rely on the phone, and at the stations where requests are considered worth looking at, the music director often makes up a form for the DJs to write that information down and keeps track of it on a weekly basis to see what the hottest request items are.

10. Maintains an up-to-date information file, and keeps press releases about artists (sometimes sent by record companies as biographical data, called *bios*) in case any questions about a group or artist arise. This is most helpful for the production director, the person responsible for doing the station's commercials. If the sponsor is a record company or a concert promoter, it helps the production director to be able to get some information about the artist or group before writing a commercial. Having bios or artist information around is also useful when listeners call to ask about a song you just played.

11. Watches the club scene, to find out what records are popular (some MDs do record hops or dances and derive that information in the process), as well as what records get the most reaction. What songs do people seem to prefer to dance to? What records get them out on the floor, and what records bore them? Granted, radio isn't like a dance club, but the more information you have about your audience, the better you will be able to adjust your programming to make them happy. For that reason too, as we mentioned earlier, a wise MD also observes the latest trends and fads, making sure a particular trend relates to the station's target audience, and, otherwise, ignores it.

12. Lets the PD know which artists are coming to town, in case a promotion or an interview can be planned around this. Record companies are a good resource for artist tour itineraries, but certain music magazines and MTV also provide this information.

13. At stations which have the music library on computer, compiles the daily playlists, making changes to the data as needed. More and more stations have replaced manual music selection with putting it on computer. At stations where the music is still in card files, the MD makes sure the cards are up to date, filled out correctly, and plyed in the proper sequence. MDs type up new cards or replace old ones as needed. In either system, the music director is responsible for making sure the format is being executed the right way and that all songs are in their proper category. (As early Top-40 PDs had found out the hard way, not all songs have equal value. Some are more important than others and are in categories that enable them to be repeated more frequently.) Some MDs actually police the format; that is, they listen at random and see if in fact the DJs are playing what they are supposed to play. A common problem at small-market stations (and at some bigger ones too) is that weekend DJs, who are often new, don't do the format right. Some don't understand how to, while others feel some of their own favorite songs should be included. In either case, the MD often helps the PD by training the new announcers in how to do the format and then makes sure only the approved songs are played.

14. Answers questions from listeners (and sometimes staff) about the music. As early music librarians were often the resident experts, so are many of today's music directors. They answer trivia challenges, settle friendly bets, or identify the name of a song the listener heard 6 weeks ago and the only fact the person recalls is that the song had the word "love" in the title. Sometimes MDs are asked by members of the sales department to provide a suitable background song for a client's commercial or are asked to explain why a certain record is being played on the station. Often, listeners call and ask where a certain song can be bought; this is especially common at AOR, where certain rare records or foreign imports are played. These calls are often routed to the MD.

To sum up, these and more, are the duties of the music director. The job has become a lot more challenging over the years, especially with new technologies and more emphasis on research. Next, some advice about how to be more effective as a music director.

7

Music Directing in the 1990s

It was probably much easier to be a music director 20 years ago. For one thing, there were fewer radio stations competing for the same audience. For another, AM radio stations, many of which did Top-40, remained powerful in most cities, despite the inroads FM and Progressive Rock had made. Back in 1970, Top-40 music directors (and many in other formats, although Progressive Rock by now had a few trades of its own, as did Black and Country) looked at *Billboard* and *Record World*; some also read *Cashbox*, although this trade was still regarded as mainly a jukebox-oriented publication. *The Gavin Report* had been published since Top-40's early days and was still seen as an honest and highly ethical trade which reviewed the new releases fairly. Many MDs found Bill Gavin's reviews useful, and station management read and quoted from his thought-provoking editorials.

In Canada, where many young people who lived close enough to the U.S. border listened to the American stations, there was only one trade, *RPM*. The majority of Canadian Top-40 stations either used the U.S. trades or, in the case of stations like CHUM in Toronto, did their own charts, based on local sales and research; a number of Canadian Top-40s relied on CHUM's playlist as a reference point for their own music selections. FM was slow to become a haven for Progressive Rock, so a few of Canada's best rock groups were trying to get airplay on the U.S. stations, in hopes of having that one big hit which would get Canadian Top-40 to play their songs. Meanwhile, the Canadian government was in the midst of dramatically intervening in the way radio was done, passing regulations that would mandate a certain percentage of Canadian music on each station. More on that later, but the point is, at the beginning of the 1970s, Canadian stations were usually influenced by the hits on the U.S. charts.

By the 1980s, so much was different in both countries. With all the changes came a new set of problems and challenges for PDs and MDs. One big change, of course, was that music had moved almost entirely to FM in the United States (which was not totally the case in Canada, where government regulations assured AM of survival. Still, even in Canada, Album Rock and Adult Contemporary became fixtures on the FM band) and new formats on AM stressed talk or news. Some AM stations played Oldies, and Black, Traditional Country, and specialized formats such as all Folk Music or all Gospel found a niche. But in general, American listeners who wanted music moved over to FM. Those PDs and MDs at AM stations that still played some music were faced with determining what music to play and how to maintain good ratings.

Another challenge was audience fragmentation. As we have seen, where once there had basically been two formats (MOR and Top-40), soon there were ten, and the ten splintered off into various permutations. For example, adults in the 25- to 44-year-old demographic could find a number of stations which played basically the same music, yet were different versions of AC: some were very hit-oriented and almost CHR, others were "Lite" and very soft, others played lots of older hits, some even mixed in some jazz or so-called New Age music. Top-40 too had its different types. The format had been renamed Contemporary Hit Radio (CHR) during a time in the early 1980s when teen music had become anathema and the push to attract adult listeners was very strong; as a result, some Top-40s sounded so wimpy that they could be mistaken for Adult Contemporary. The new name was supposed to be a positive reflection of how Top-40 had matured, but to some frustrated PDs and MDs, it only proved that there was no Top-40 anymore, just a safe, boring amalgam of pop hits and some nonoffensive dance music. But by the late 1980s, even with its new name still intact, CHR had gone back to its roots. Some CHRs were Urban-flavored, playing the new dance and Black hits first; others were rock-oriented, avoiding dance hits and stressing songs that crossed over from Album Rock. These so-called Rock-40 stations weren't afraid to be loud, and they weren't worried about having a young audience. Another type of CHR also made use of Top-40's once outrageous image. Stations calling themselves "the Power Pig" and "Pirate Radio" featured controversial DJs, on morning shows (often called "the Morning Zoo"). They sometimes told off-color or offensive jokes along with playing the latest hits— a promotional effort that concentrated on creating a rebellious, bad boy stance. Some parents and church groups were outraged by these stations, claiming they were ob-scene. But as with any controversy, the more the adults complained, the more young people wanted to listen to see what all the fuss was about.

So, with as many as five types of CHR, numerous types of AC, Pop/Urban (stations that played some white dance hits) versus Black/Urban (stations that wouldn't play anything unless it was on the black charts), Traditional Country versus Modern Country, and so much more, listeners in many cities felt overwhelmed. Researchers found that these listeners were confused about what stations they had listened to, since they felt so many sounded alike. They also noted that listeners could not specify one favorite station; most listened to three or four. There were just too many choices. This made life very difficult for PDs and MDs who, years ago, just had to play the hits and ben entertaining. Now, in such an over-radioed universe, stations had to come up with positioning strategies so that listeners would remember what they had been listening to and tell the ratings companies when the question was asked. (another change was that many cities which had only had one rating period a year now had two; some had as many as four, which meant that it was more impor-tant than ever to make an impression on the audience.) PDs and MDs now found that they had to invent new slogans and new methods of highlighting the music, as well as finding ways to make their station stand out.

There were other complications for radio. Listener loyalty had certainly eroded: if all stations sounded virtually alike to the passive listener, why choose any one in particular? The days when the family gathered around their one favorite station to hear the singers they loved were long gone; today's audience had grown up with

Top-40, and they had become accustomed to hit songs, no matter who sang them; they grew restless when they didn't hear songs they liked. Then there was the fact that the audience had a much shorter attention span than that of previous generations. For one thing, they didn't read as much; they watched TV. For another, demographers found that especially in the 25- to 44-year-old age group, people felt overworked and pressed for time. The economy was sluggish in many cities, women were back in the work force, and middle-class families felt they needed two incomes just to be able to make ends meet. Leisure time was at a premium, and going to a movie or taking the family to a nice restaurant was out of the question for many. This made in-home entertainment even more important, since it cost so much to go out. More homes got cable TV, which offered not only movies but music videos. Many also had a VCR so that if radio or TV became boring, they could shut it off entirely and rent a film.

Radio programmers reacted to the needs of the audience. Newscasts were shortened and made more concise; critics complained that this also made the coverage superficial, but research showed repeatedly that people just did not have as much time and they wanted their information quickly. More AC stations began to run contests, offering listeners money to ay their bills. Music directors saw a new importance placed on celebrity news: the average listener was curious about the exploits of some of music's more outrageous members, and as a result, vignettes about such people as Madonna, Boy George, or Ozzy Osbourne were blended into newscasts along with hard news. The way store research had been done also changed. In years previous, it had been assumed that only teens bought records, and they mainly bought hit singles. With the single a dying configuration by the late 1980s, store research was now based on cassette and compact disc sales; in markets with many dance clubs, the sales of 12-inch dance mixes were also looked at. But PDs and MDs had to reevaluate their beliefs about the adult audience, for research showed that these 25- to 44-year-olds, who had changed radio so dramatically when they were teens in the 1950s, still loved music. Although they didn't buy as much as teens did, they did go into record stores. Many went to replace an old, much played album with a new compact disc version; but just as many went to purchase new releases by artists with adult appeal, such as Basia or Bonnie Raitt. MDs at AC and Adult CHR stations found that it was in their best interest to be aware of what these adults liked.

The 25- to 44-year-old age group also made its impact on Album Rock. In the past, it had been commonly believed that once a teenager grew into adulthood, that adult would no longer want to hear rock music. The so-called baby boomers were different, however. Not only did they still like rock, but they still wanted it as part of their lives. Of course, some adults did opt for softer music, but large numbers of them remained loyal to the music of their teenaged years. This made the Oldies format very popular, but it also affected AOR. Album stations found that teens of the 1980s wanted the hard edged, so-called heavy metal form of rock. But adults liked the rock they had grown up with: Led Zeppelin, Cream, The Who, Bob Seger, and others. This evolved into a format known as Classic Rock, and it became very successful. The PDs and MDs who anticipated this trend were able to position their station as either a Classic Rocker or a mainstream AOR, depending on which one their market lacked.

So, with all the challenges and potential pitfalls, what can a good MD do to help his or her station remain competitive? I suggest the following.

1. Be aware of all kinds of music, not just what you personally like or only what your station plays. If your station is hit-oriented, you may end up playing a record that crossed over from Reggae or Jazz/Fusion or MOR. Also, expectations of formats change. Years ago, there was a very rigid definition of what an Ac station could play, where today, many ACs can and do play music that might have been considered too hard in the past. The more you know, the more valuable you are to your PD and to the audience. Also, from a pragmatic standpoint, the more you know, the more you may save your job. Stations do change formats. Years ago, with less competition and less emphasis on ratings, a PD or MD could specialize in only one format and there was no problem. But with so many stations acquiring new owners or facing new competitors, a versatile MD is often a still-employed MD. In my own music directing career, I once had to move from Album Rock to MOR. I was glad I had kept up with both.

2. Understand how a record becomes a hit. It's a much more complicated process now. As we discussed earlier, at one time there were just a few releases, and these tended to be by big-name artists. Songs became popular thanks to jukebox play, placement on a network radio show, and the enthusiasm of certain major announcers such as Martin Block. As MOR gave way to Top-40, and as sheet music gave way to singles sales, the support of key DJs remained crucial for a song to become a hit. Song pluggers were now record promoters, and there was no longer a small group of influential band leaders or announcers; Top-40 spread rapidly, and a number of important DJs emerged as a result. Today, long before a music director ever receives a new release, the record companies have done lots of behind-the-scenes planning. It all begins when a group is signed by the company, after having been seen by the Artists & Repertoire department and then approved by the entire staff. It is A & R's responsibility to find artists with hit potential. Once these artists have been signed, they go into the studio to record. The completed product is then played for the heads of promotion, marketing, sales, and publicity; these record executives will decide what the first single will be, and they will also develop a strategy to promote the new group. Of course, in selecting that all-important first single, the company also receives input from the band itself along with its management so that a unified plan can be created. Though 45s no longer sell well, the idea of a hit single is still essential: that one track will be the public's first introduction to the new group. Today, cassette singles are very popular, so the company will plan the artwork, decide if any promotional items will accompany the release of the record (sometimes posters, key chains, T-shirts, or buttons are sent to radio PDs and MDs along with the release, with the idea of making that particular record stand out amid all the others radio stations receive in any given week), and make certain that enough copies of the release are in the record stores. Meetings are held at the local offices in each city so that the field staff is aware of the new group and understands what the plan for promoting them is. The vice president of promotion, who works out of the company's home office in most cases, will oversee the local staff and coordinate all promotional activity. The local promoters will visit all the key stations in their terri-

tory, and they will call in how many stations added the record so that the vice president of promotion can chart the record's progress.

Michael Plen, vice president of promotion for Virgin Records, told me it can often take a commitment of hundreds of thousands of dollars to break a new artist. "Many radio people have no idea all the groundwork a record company has to undertake in order to make a record a hit. It's like building something: you get one station to believe in the record, then another, and another, and you keep on building it that way. Getting enough radio airplay is the key. Obviously, not every record of ours will be a hit, even when it does get airplay. But in so many cases, that airplay was what made the difference."

The record business today is very lucrative, and the boom in compact disc sales has made it even more so. CDs, which are more expensive than albums, can generate a profit of as much as $6 for the labels, nearly double the profit they made on albums. (Cynics have accused the labels of phasing out albums not because CDs sound better but because there is more money to be made on them. Although consumers have complained about the price of CDs, which are sold for about $16 typically, the price hasn't dropped much, nor have albums made a comeback.)

Why should a music director know or care about any of this? The more aware an MD is about the hit-making process, the less likely the chance of being fooled by a record with no hit potential but lots of promotional dollars behind it. Also, since MDs interact so often with record reps, it never hurts to understand their job and the pressures they are under. Beware of the promoter who tells you every week that jobs are on the line unless a certain record is added. While sometimes that may be true, in most cases, good promoters are not expected to get every record played nor are they penalized for not doing so.

3. Don't be afraid to take a chance. Perhaps up to this point, it seemed as if the message to music directors was "only play the hits." While making the passives happy is a worthy goal, especially in tightly restricted formats such as CHR, that doesn't mean your station has to play "follow the leader." As a consultant, I certainly advocate being careful of what you add; playing records that just don't fit your station's total sound can alienate potential listeners. but I ams also a firm believer in keeping your station's sound fresh and interesting. While many college stations today are free-form (today called Alternative) and play anything as long as it's different from mass-appeal radio, out in the world of professional radio, stations have a certain structure that must be respected. That structure does not prevent a good MD from exposing new music; it simply assures the audience that the music mix will never become so extreme that listeners won't feel at ease. There have always been PDs and MDs at the tightest Top-40 stations who believed in certain records and went out on a limb for them. Numerous songs that failed their first time out were re-released and went on to be hits because such PDs and MDs got behind the record and gave it a second chance. As long as a new song is surrounded by familiar and proven hits, I see no evidence that it is dangerous to play something unfamiliar. My earliest memories of Top-40 are of the innovative DJs (back when it was they who picked the hits) like Arnie Ginsberg and Dick Summer who were not afraid to give a new artist a chance. There are many stories about courageous MDs who were ahead of their time, such as the Top-40 MD at a station in Philadelphia who thought an

artist named Bruce Springsteen had hit potential, even though he was mainly an Album Rocker back then. Today, that MD, Joel Denver, is the influential CHR editor at *Radio & Records*, where he still gives his opinion about new artists and is often ahead of everyone in recognizing a hit. Unusual and unique songs, such as "Baker Street" by Gerry Rafferty, "Total Eclipse of the Heart" by Bonnie Tyler, and "Red Red Wine" by UB 40 demonstrated admirably that just because your format is CHR, you can still play something creative. That opportunity to be creative exists in every format. Some very conservative AOR stations were responsible for the success of U2, INXS, and the Cure, among others. Yes, college radio played them first, but the mass audience, that large number of musically unsophisticated listeners, became familiar with these bands when their local AOR added them. So, it was a partnership in a way: college stations helped call attention to these bands, and then AOR took the next step, and everyone benefited. If the next generation of interesting artists, those like Sinéad O'Connor in AOR, Basia in AC, the so-called New Traditionalists like Clint Black in Country, rap artists like M. C. Hammer, and so many more are to get the airplay they deserve, it will take MDs with good ears who know what fits their format but who also know what might provide an exciting change of pace.

4. Manage your time well. If you don't happen to be a very organized person, being a music director may force you to change. Juggling record calls, handling an airshift, contacting the trades, keeping the library in order, working on the computer or typing cards, and still trying to listen to all the new releases can be stressful if you aren't careful. At the risk of sounding like your mom, make sure you're healthy. It's difficult enough to manage stress, but if you let yourself get run down, you'll make the job twice as difficult. No matter how much you love radio, don't spend all your time at the station, or you'll never meet any of your listening audience, and you won't know what music they like. The best music directors know their market. If you don't, you should. Learn how to cut down on interruptions, and keep a list of what you expect to accomplish each day. If all else fails, attend a seminar in time management: a number of companies offer them, as do many colleges. If you can't find the time to do that, read a book on the subject. You can't be effective today unless you are organized. And, how's your attitude these days? Is life amusing to you or is it tedious and aggravating? We all have our bad days, but if every day is full of events that make you furious, the chances are your work is being affected, as well as any personal life you might have. If it's been a while since you've enjoyed anything, it's definitely time to stop and reevaluate so that you can make a positive contribution again instead of feeling as if nobody appreciates what you do. It may be time for a job change; it may be time to take a day off. But look honestly at how you manage your time, and if you don't like what you see, take steps to correct it.

5. Be careful out there. Several controversial issues have resurfaced over the past few years. One is about so-called obscene lyrics in songs. The other involves certain trends that supposedly have a negative impact on young people, namely, hard-rock music and rap music. Since you are a department head, and since you represent the radio station's music policy, it's in your best interest to think about these subjects.

In the late 1980s, a group of influential women, wives of U.S. senators, began a committee to combat what they felt were dangerous song lyrics that might have a detrimental effect on young people. As you know, this is not new: for generations, various church and civic groups have accused popular music of everything from obscenity to satanism. The current outcry has become a political issue in some states, and now those states are attempting to pass legislation to place warning stickers on records felt to have controversial lyrics. In some states, local politicians, sensing a hot issue, have tried to pass laws restricting the sale of certain records to those under 18 years old. Former Governor Bob Martinez of Florida told *U.S. News & World Report* that he regards certain songs as "audio pornography" and wants those who make these records, as well as those who sell them, prosecuted. On the other side of the issue are numerous artists and civil libertarians who feel that declaring a song obscene is a subjective judgment and clearly violates free speech protections under the First Amendment. As I write this, some record companies have voluntarily stickered certain CDs as "containing material not suitable for children," or given a "parental advisory" warning. Certain artists feel that even this smacks of censorship, and several have put their own warning sticker on their new releases, warning prudes or censors not to buy them. Interestingly, one rap group which was the subject of much of the controversy about obscene lyrics, 2 Live Crew, ended up selling several million copies of the very record that was supposedly obscene.

Wherever you stand personally on the issue isn't as important as the fact that your station's license promises that the station will operate in the public interest. Different communities have different standards, but you must know what would be offensive in your market. I personally do not believe in censorship, but I do believe in being mature and responsible about my job. As an MD, you must be prepared to handle irate listener calls if they arise. You must take these callers seriously, even if you don't agree with them. Be respectful and have a logical explanation for your station's music policy. I don't expect you to pull every record that some listener objects to, and if you feel the song in question is worth playing, then take a stand for it. But never ignore these callers, or they may then complain to the FCC. The lyrics controversy is especially problematic because some songs that certain groups are protesting have been badly misinterpreted. For example, Ozzy Osbourne's "Suicide Solution" is *not* telling kids to kill themselves, yet some church groups have come to believe that is exactly what Ozzy advocates. Some songs are indeed heavy on sexual innuendo, or seem to have a pro-drugs stance, but my advice to MDs is to use common sense. There will always be somebody who doesn't approve of certain songs (I once had a client who wanted every song that said "making love" removed from the library because he felt they were dirty); and to me, sometimes it isn't worth the aggravation to play them. Ask yourself if the song will make your station sound better and would you even consider playing it if it weren't controversial. The, do what you feel is the best thing, both for the station and for the audience. Don't lose sight of the fact that radio has always played songs about controversial subjects and will probably continue. Pop music has tackled some serious subjects: child abuse (Pat Benatar's "Hell is for Children" and Suzanne Vega's "Luka" are two examples), alcoholism (contrary to the stereotype that all Country songs are about drinking or cheating, there have been some very sensitive antidrinking songs that became hits; one of my favorites was T.G. Sheppard's "Devil in the Bottle"), prejudice (for every antigay or antiblack song, there have also been songs that criticized bigotry). It's not always the subject matter that creates the controversy. Some songs do seem to go out of their way to offend. Is it censorship not to play them? I don't think so, because people are still free to buy them at a record store. So, pay close attention to the music you play; you may have to defend it.

One final point about the censorship controversy. Many writers have stated that they feel the real issue is racism, since it has been mainly black rap groups who have received most of the criticism. But certain hard rock and heavy metal band,s who ar white, have also come in for their share of complaints too. Both heavy metal and rap are genres aimed at youth. They often carry a rebellious message, as youth-oriented music has for generations. Today, because of changing social standards, certain so-called street language (like the "seven words you aren't supposed to say on the radio") is regularly heard in movies. Even TV, which had very conservative standards for many years, allows certain words that were not commonly used even a decade ago. Still, the FCC and various groups concerned with morality do monitor both radio and TV. For me, the problem is more about language than about color. While I support anyone's right of self-expression, I'm not comfortable playing songs that use blatant and vulgar descriptions of sex, talk about doing violence to women or gays, or otherwise utilize extreme shock tactics. Not all rap and metal artists do this, nor are all their songs crude. So, if your format can make use of either genre, by all means, play them. But keep in mind that maybe the world won't end if your station simply ignores "Me So Horny."

6. Let's take the complexity out of music directing. All too many stations worry about ratings so much that they have become fearful of taking any chances at all. There has been an increasing amount of pressure on record promoters as well as music directors, and many told me they feel their work has been turned into a huge numbers game. Some MDs feel overwhelmed with all the choices and niches. Consider the trades: today, MDs receive a wide array, from old reliable *Billboard* to newer trades like *Pulse of Radio* and *Monday Morning Replay*. Most get *Radio & Records*; one of Top-40's first trades, *The Gavin Report* remains alive and well, and the staff of the now-defunct *Record World* surfaced at *Hits Magazine*, and so on. There are tip sheets (publications which mainly review new records and predict the hits) for CHR, such as Kal Rudman's *Friday Morning Quarterback* and Bobby Poe's *Pop Music Survey*. both Rudman and Poe have long histories in Top-40/CHR: Rudman worked at *Record World* during the 1970s and was known for his knowledge of R & B and Black crossover, while Poe was a musician and songwriter in the South and was involved with several hit groups. (Today, Poe is also known for his annual CHR convention, where PDs and MDs mingle with what seems like every record promoter who ever lived, for a weekend of panel discussions and festivities. It has its sexist moments, but it's reputable and a good place to meet people from the CHR end of the industry.) There are also trades and tip sheets for AC (such as *Inside Radio*, *Radio Only* and *Radio Business Report*. Some interesting celebrity news can be found in *One to One*, along with useful discussion about doing your airshift better. I haven't listed half of the currently available publications!

It was so much easier way back in the days before rock, there was one chart only, *The Accurate*. It basically listed what songs were played at night on the networks, and publishers used it to check up on their song pluggers. Next came *The Peatman*, created by a New York professor. It gave more information that *The Accu-*

rate, and offered a weekly Top-50 based on which highly rated shows played which songs. As for *Billboard*, it didn't yet pay much attention to popular music. It was originally published for people in vaudeville and theater, and it didn't begin publishing its now famous *Hot 100* chart until 1958. If you live and work in Canada, you not only have access to all the U.S. trades, but also *RPM* is still around as is a more recent and widely read publication called *The Record*. Since Canada has specific rules about how much Canadian music (CanCon) stations must play, MDs read the trades carefully: the two Canadian trades list which songs meet the CanCon requirements. Interestingly the rules also allow AM stations to play the hits more frequently than FM station can.

So how can an already stressed out MD decide which trade are the best ones? Since I love to read, I can usually find something interesting in all of them; but if your time is limited, seek out the trades that not only review records but also have information about your format and your target audience. Most MDs today read *R & R* faithfully. *Gavin* is also popular, but every trade has its own supporters. Record companies look closely at those stations which are reporters, as we have discussed elsewhere. While everyone involved usually denies it, *R & R* reporters seem to get the best service, with *Gavin* and *Billboard* reporters next. Some trades are willing to let any subscriber report, but others are very selective. To become a reporter requires good ratings and/or a positive station image, including a well-organized music department. Many stations apply to become *R & R* reporters (parallels), but only a few will be chosen. MDs who aren't *R & R* reporters should develop a good relationship with a trade to which they can report and build from that. If you are a reliable and articulate spokesperson for your station and you keep in touch with the record companies, you will probably get good record service. But as we discussed before, in some cities the parallels seem to be treated better than those stations which aren't. For example, parallels often attract bigger promotions (such as trips to a major city to meet a rock star). No record company wants to offend any station that reports to a trade, however, during my experience music directing, as well as in conversations I had with MDs, we often perceived that the *Gavin* and *Billboard* reporters got smaller prizes for giveaways—a box of cassettes, for example. Before you say, wait a minute, isn't that payola, the rule is that stations can in fact accept a box of cassettes, concert tickets, or whatever as long as there is no link between the gift and any airplay, and as long as the station gives regular on-air identification that says they got the item from a record company.) You've heard this many times, as a DJ will say "call me up and win the new Madonna CD, *promotional consideration Warner Brothers Records*"), while *R & R* reporters got better prizes or got specially made artist IDs ("Hi, this is Madonna, and whenever I'm in Yourtown, I listen to Magic 109.". While this doesn't occur in every market, the fact remains that being a reporter carries status.

As for how busy MDs can still have fun, I'd like to see a return to the days when radio wasn't so dominated by the bottom line. Yes, radio is a business and should be run like one, but when my record promoter friends talk about promotion as being a game of statistics today, I can empathize. Promotion used to be about personalities—many successful promoters were unique characters who weren't afraid to be outrageous in order to get a record played; and by outrageous, I don't mean illegal. I've had record reps call on me dressed up in a gorilla costume, or on roller skates;

two of them once descended on my office dressed as member of the Mob—they were "hit men," of course. One rep brought along fake handcuffs to one music call and threatened to chain himself to my office door if I didn't add his record. While not all reps today are totally serious, I do see less of that clowning around. Today, music calls are about facts and figures: how many adds the song got, what its position is on the R & R charts, etc. With the emphasis on research at many stations, more concrete proof of a record's potential is sought, as opposed to the days when MDs added a song just because they had a feeling it would be a hit. Matt Hudson, an executive with Mid-continent Broadcasting in Madison, Wisconsin, told me, "I used to enjoy being a music director. It was abut being the ears for the entire market. During the 70s, music directors had a lot of input; and record promotion was a lot more creative. But then in the 1980s, the industry changed. It became more corporate. With the emphasis on the bottom line, everyone was expected to deliver *now*. As a result, there was more pressure, and music directing stopped being fun." But Hudson sees more changes in the 1990s. "Today's MDs should use the trades and research as tools, but they are not the bible. And record companies will have to release fewer records and commit themselves to more accurate priorities. Then music directing can return to being about picking the hits."

Author and respected lecturer David J. Rogers agrees. In a speech to a recent *Radio & Records* convention in Los Angeles he told the audience that as he saw it, there would be a trend in the 1990s toward fewer releases and fewer artists per label, with the emphasis being on breaking new talent. Noting how conservative some stations have become about adding records, Rogers said, "Radio will continue to be records' main method to expose an artist to a large audience. However, because [some stations have been adding so few new records] record companies will [also use] word of mouth, in-store selling, increased video action, and showcases."

7. Learn to work with consultants, music software, and other elements of today's radio, even if they seem restrictive to you. Research is not going to go away. While some stations may have relied too heavily on it, to the exclusion of their staff's good instincts, PDs and MDs can certainly benefit from knowing more about the likes and dislikes of the audience. As for computers, more and more stations are using them. The new generation of software is much easier to understand, and much more user-friendly. Even if you prefer to mix your own musical sets, the reality is that many managers like the consistency a computer can bring. Having it available to schedule and rotate the music frees the MD to do other things. Virtually every computer software package includes an editing function, so if you see a set of songs that really doesn't look right to you, it is possible to make changes before a final music list is printed. Perhaps the best-known of all the music selection systems is called Selector; it was the original and is used all over the world. Selector's chief competition comes from MusicScan, and Generation II, which are also effective. These systems may be too expensive for small-market stations, and there are other established companies who offer music software that is aimed at the needs of the smaller station. The benefit of these systems is that the computer can keep track of your rotations, avoid playing too much of a certain artist, and make sure no songs are overlooked just because a certain DJ didn't like them. Computerized music selection today is seen as a more efficient method than using card files.

As for consultants, some people regard them as a negative, but they too are here to stay and have been for several decades. The stereotype of the consultant is that he or she comes in and fires people or never lets the staff have any say. While there have certainly been instances of that, I've found that consultants vary in style, just like PDs or MDs do. In some cases, the tight control the consultant maintains is what the station management has requested. One of radio's best-known consultants, Kent Burkhart, at one time worked in partnership with AOR expert Lee Abrams. That combo, Burkhart/Abrams & Associates, was the most powerful consultancy of the 1970s, with clients from coast to coast. Burkhart looked back on consulting AOR in those transitional days when the format was trying to shed its hippie image and become more mass-appeal. "Back in the 1970s, AOR was still a fairly new format, so owners wanted us to have total control. They didn't want to leave anything to chance. In fact, since it was usually the GM or even the company president who brought us in, they *expected* us to have that degree of control. I understood their reasoning: most of their PDs and MDs were either new to the format or inexperienced in programming. In fact, in those early days of Album Rock, many of the stations didn't even have a music director. They just had a PD who often guessed what music should be played. PDs back then were not as knowledgeable or as skilled as they are today." Basically, the PD and MD had little or no autonomy under the Burkhart/Abrams system. The two provided client stations with a playlist based on research. New records were added weekly, but Lee and Kent supervised the adds and had the last word. The PDs weren't totally ignored: there was a music call each week, and at that time, they could make suggestions or lobby in favor of a particular record. "The record promoters would come to our office [in Atlanta] on Mondays and play us their latest releases. They had our total attention from 8 A.M.. to 10 A.M., after which , we'd make up our minds." It certainly must have been a major coup for any record promoter when Burkhart/Abrams did decide to add a particular album; that approval could mean as many as 100 stations would be playing it.

Today, while Burkhart and Abrams no longer work together, both are still influential, as are a number of other consultants, some of whom specialize in one certain format. Rusty Walker is one of the best known Country consultants. He oversees the music selection at all his client stations but relies on the PD and MD to know what will sound good in their market. "If we have to do the music for them," says Walker, "then they don't need a consultant; they need a new PD. I don't think a consultant should have total control over a station's music: that's not a healthy situation." On the other hand, Walker believes in the necessity for PDs and MDs to be aware and informed. On weekly music calls, he and his associates discuss the music, talking to each PD and MD about songs that are going well in research, songs that people seem tired of, what other key stations have added, and what the national charts show about certain songs. But Walker still expects client PDs and MDs to express their ideas and beliefs and know how to do their job effectively so that a consultant won't have to do it for them. "I see a consultant's role as that of a sounding board; we can provide an objective overview and keep the station on track."

My advice to new MDs is don't automatically assume that just because your station is consulted, you won't get a chance to give any input. At the stations I consult, and I believe this is true of most consultants, I tend to give a lot of direction to PDs and MDs who are not yet familiar with the job, but as we work together for a while and they show me that they know what they are doing, I take their opinions into account more and more. Like anything else, a consultant/client relationship is built on trust. Since my role is to oversee and improve the station's sound, I prefer PDs and MDs who are honest with e and who don't let their own personal musical tastes interfere with what the audience wants. Despite all the horror stories about consultants, most have useful information you can derive from them. In most cases, talent will be rewarded: even back in the days when Burkhart/Abrams was calling so many of the shots, creative and talented PDs and MDs were moved up to bigger stations and given more authority.

Perhaps by now you are wondering why I haven't yet named some of the industry's best MDs. I have two reasons: realistically, by the time a book goes to press, some of those people may be with other stations or may be out of work; and, since I have great respect for so many MDs, I'm reticent to single out a chosen few, because I don't want to unintentionally overlook someone who deserves a mention. But I would like to acknowledge the great ears of such people as Sunny Joe White, John Lander, Guy Zapolean, Keith Naftaly, Dena Yasner, and Oedipus; people like them keep radio interesting.

Many successful PDs of today were at one time music directors. But how do people decide to music direct? I received a variety of answers from the people I interviewed. As I mentioned earlier, many of the best MDs got their start in college radio. (Interestingly, so did many of today's best record executives who enjoyed music directing but decided they preferred the records aspect of the industry more than radio. Those record executives who never did college radio got their start in local branches of distributors, working in the warehouse and learning the business from the ground up.) A number of former college MDs admitted that they found the job by accident; but once they began doing it, they decided to stay with it. As for other ways of entering the realm of music directing, Bob Cummings, a former GM in Las Vegas who now owns a station in Phoenix was originally ba booking agent, hiring DJs to do local dances and booking bands for small concerts. He was a DJ while in the service (where one of his best memories was meeting a then-unknown musician named Elton John), and when he returned to the United State, he sought a radio job where he could utilize his knowledge of music. That led him to music directing and he did so for several large Top-40 stations in Hartford and Providence during the 1970s.

Another industry executive, Ed Salamon, is president of Unistar Communications, but he too became a music director first. Actually, the MD job came after he spent some time in Pittsburgh at KDKA as the director of marketing and research. But he became fascinated with programming, and that led him to the station's music department. KDKA at that time was a Full-Service AC with a basically older audience. "When I became music director in the early 80s, management had decided that we needed to attract a somewhat younger audience. My job was to gradually lower our demographics without offending all our listeners. So, I started removing all the old MOR music and moved KDKA in a more AC direction. But I got some resistance from a few of the older announcers, who didn't agree with the changes. They even tried to bring in their favorite records from home when they thought I wasn't around." Salamon was around more than they had expected, however, and soon the new format was implemented and adhered to. It also became very successful, and Salamon moved up to program directing.

Some MDs have worked into the job from interning at a station. When I was in college, I was one of several students who answered the request line and did errands for the DJs at a local station. While in my case, it never led to full-time work, I made some good contacts and established my credibility as a knowledgeable music person. I have seen such jobs eventually lead to something full-time if the person was enthusiastic and willing to learn the station's system. I realize that today some people choose not to do volunteer work and of course a paying job is usually what students seek, but volunteering at a radio station does provide some on-the-job experience that might not be achieved otherwise.

Some of the present and former MDs with whom I spoke had words of advice for anyone interested in being a successful music director. Jim Smith, today a respected consultant, at one time was music director for then Top-40 giant WLS in Chicago. Like its sister station in New York, WABC, the station had a very tight playlist, added few records, and was known for its honesty even during the payola scandal. Smith recalls his music directing days in the early 1970s. "At WLS, we had music by committee. While the final choice was up to me and the program director, the GM and the sales manager would sit in on the weekly music meeting. No records were played at those meetings, however. Basically, I would present to everyone there the research on the songs I thought we should add, as well as explaining the reasons for adding them. We always had a lot of information available because I called over 100 sales locations every week. In general, we only added two songs a week. We looked at the song's national chart action, considered if it was a core artist for us, and since we didn't do any call-out research in those days, I used my gut feel as to whether or not a song was right for WLS. Our main competition, WCFL, played a lot of Urban, so we positioned ourselves as more rock- and adult-oriented than they were."

What can be learned from Jim Smith's experience at WLS is that a job which on the surface seems very restrictive can evolve. When it became obvious to him that doing store research was necessary but time-consuming, Smith developed a system for computer tabulating the information. Also, he knew that in order to get anything added to WLS, he would have to be responsible for building a case and defending his choices. This made him approach his work in an organized manner so that when he was called upon at the music meeting, he would be ready.

When Bob Cummings was a music director, he too saw the structure in the job, but he made that structure work positively for the audience. "The reason I was good at music directing was that I never played the records I personally liked. I played what I knew the listeners wanted to hear." Cummings had an interesting way of determining if a song was really popular, which he had learned from his days as a booking agent. "I'd go and listen to the local bands, and whatever songs they were covering, I knew those must be the hits, because cover bands only perform the best-known material. And I also made sure to check what songs people played on the jukebox."

In addition to learning to separate your personal favorites from the music that' right for your station and acquiring self-discipline about the job's limitations, Professor Michael Keith recommends a realistic attitude about professional radio. Keith has written a number of respected texts on broadcasting and has been an active supporter of college radio. He spoke about why some college MDs fail to succeed in professional radio.

> I don't believe most college stations prepare students for the real world. Most are doing some form of Alternative Rock, where the D.J.'s pick their own music, nobody has to play anything mass-appeal, and "format" is a dirty word. In some colleges, the campus station is just another student activity, and the students do what they want: you might have one show that's all jazz, another that's all new age, or heavy metal, or whatever. The student can bring in their own records because there are no guidelines. And since some of the faculty advisors to these stations know very little about radio, and may even have contempt for commercial radio, the students are never prepared for how to work with a format. In fact, they may even get the impression that they shouldn't have to work with one. That's why while I was at Dean Junior College, we set up a CHR station. I'm sure the students wished they could play obscure music, but I felt that wouldn't help them to eventually get a job in the industry. WGAO is run as if it were a professional operation: the faculty advisor is an experienced radio person with a CHR background and he picks the music. Students may make suggestions at the music meeting, just as they might at a professional station. But they have to follow the format, and they can't play whatever they feel like playing. We even have hot clocks, a computer that generates playlists, and typical CHR music rotations. I do know a few college stations that have a specific format, but I think we're all in the minority. Most college stations don't give the students the discipline they'll need to do the job successfully out in the real world.

And then, there are some pet peeves that MDs and record promoters have. Many MDs I interviewed said they wished the GM would stay out of the music selection; unfortunately, at some stations, especially in smaller markets, the GM is a former PD who still misses programming and at times wants to get back to it. Usually, it's just on occasion, but I do know a few stations where the GM, or even the owner, tries to insert certain of their own favorite songs into the rotation. I advise MDs when this happens to try to discuss it in a calm and nonthreatening manner, since putting your boss on the defensive probably won't win you the argument. Show the GM that while you certainly appreciate the input, you feel the songs he or she wants to add aren't right for the station and would do more harm than good. Most GMs can see that, although at times it may require a word from someone else, like your consultant, to get the message across. On the other hand, some GMs are very musically aware and can offer some good suggestions. Kemosabi Joe (Joe Johnson) was PD and MD of Z104 in Frederick, Maryland; the station had a reputation for breaking new artists. While Joe did the lion's share of the station's programming, he did the music with his GM, (The Real) Howard Johnson. I asked him if that was a problem. "It wasn't really a problem. Howard never made me feel as if I had no authority. The fact was that he was a very knowledgeable guy. So we were really partners. He never stopped me from doing my job, and even when we disagreed, we always respected each other."

Gene Knight, MD of influential AC station B100 in San Diego discussed one of his pet peeves in an article by *R & R*'s AC editor, Mike Kinosian. As a music director with a lot of autonomy, Knight regards his job as very important, and he takes great pride in doing it. But what slows him down, he says, is record companies that lack good communication with their own staff. "Sometimes, I'll get nine or ten calls in a day about the same record. That bogs me down to the point that I have to tell them I've already heard the story."

The other side of that coin is a common complaint by record promoters about how certain MDs are not totally honest. Independent promoter Tom Kay of Main Street Promotions in Minneapolis says, "So much of record promotion is about relationships. Some PDs and MDs think that if they say no [about adding a record], it will hurt the good relationship we have built. But, actually, we want to know the truth. If a record isn't right for a station, I'd rather have somebody tell me that, instead of saying they're going to add it and then mysteriously the record never gets on the air." *R & R*'s Joel Denver told me that the biggest lesson he every learned as a music director was how to say no diplomatically. It's a useful skill to have. MDs should never promise to add something just to make a record promoter stop calling.

One fairly recent problem record promoters have with radio is the assumption that the company should provide artists for station promotions. "It's not quite like payola," Tom Kay told me, "but there are certain stations that will add a record and then expect the record company to provide them with the artist for an appearance. Most companies do try to help out an important station when they can, but we can't be, nor should we be, a substitute for a station having its own promotion budget."

There is so much more to be said about music directing. Gene Knight is very proud of being an MD, and feels it's a job with a future. "I read and hear all the time that MDs are just music librarians. But as long as you have the interest, you can go forward. When you feel your hands are tied, you need to show the person you are working for how valuable you are. If you're a hard worker and a good communicator, you will gain the respect of the industry."

Someone I met years ago once told me that a hit record either makes people want to dance or makes them want to cry. Despite audience fragmentation and increased competition among cable TV, free TV and radio, music will remain an important element in the lives of most people, and radio stations will continue to seek the right combinations to get ratings and keep listeners happy. Being a good MD in the 1990s will mean keeping up with the latest fads and trends, maintaining your integrity, knowing your audience, and keeping a sense of humor. As for learning from the lessons of the past, a good person to discuss that is Juggy Gayles, a legendary record promoter who has watched it all during the over 60 years he has ben in the music industry. He was once asked about knowing what the right trends are. "I've worked with them all," he replied, "from Glenn Miller to Led Zeppelin, Woody Herman to the Eagles. It's all the same. Everybody's looking for winners, whether it's swing, disco, punk, or whatever. There ain't nothing new out there. There isn't any new wave. There's only one wave: the dance wave." That's the point: it's all about entertaining the audience. As long as there are hits to be found, good music directors will continue to find them.

Bibliography

Books

Aquila, Richard. *That Old Time Rock & Roll*. New York: Schirmer, 1989.

Baulu, Roger. *CKAC: Une Histoire d'Amour*. Montreal: Stanké, 1982.

Belz, Carl. *The Story of Rock*. New York: Oxford University Press, 1972.

Biagi, Shirley. *Media/Impact*. Belmont, California: Wadsworth, 1990.

Birkby, Robers. *KMA Radio: The First Sixty Years*. Shenandoah, Iowa: May Broadcasting, 1985.

Chapple, Steve and Reebee Garofalo, *Rock 'n' Roll Is Here to Pay*. Chicago: Nelson-Hall, 1978.

Clark, Dick. *Rock, Roll & Remember*. New York: Thomas Crowell, 1976.

Dannen, Fredric. *Hit Men*. New York: Random House, 1990.

DeLong, Thomas A. *The Mighty Music Box*. Los Angeles: Amber Crest, 1980.

Eisen, Jonathan (editor). *The Age of Rock, 2*. New York: Vintage, 1970.

Fornatale, Peter. *Radio in the Televison Age*. New York: Overlook, 1980.

Fowler, Gene and Bill Crawford. *Border Radio*. Austin: Texas Monthly Press, 1987.

Frith, Simon and Andrew Goodwin (editors). *On Record: Rock, Pop, & the Written Word*. New York: Pantheon, 1990.

Gillett, Charlie. *Making Tracks*. New York: E.P. Dutton, 1974.

Haeg, Larry, Jr. *Sixty Years Strong*. Minneapolis: WCCO Radio, 1984.

Hall, Claude and Barbara. *This Business of Radio Programming*. New York: Billboard Publications, 1977.

Jack, Donald. *Sinc, Betty and the Morning Man*. Toronto: Macmillan, 1977.

Jasen, David A. *Tin Pan Alley*. New York: Primus, 1988.

Lynch, Vincent and Henkin, Bill. *The Jukebox: The Golden Age*. New York: Putnam, 1981.

Maltin, Leonard. *Of Mice and Magic: A History of American Animated Cartoons*. rev. ed. New York: New American Library, 1987.

Morrow, Bruce. *Cousin Bruce—My Life in Rock 'n' Roll Radio*. New York: Wiliam Morrow, 1987.

Shane, Ed. *Programming Dynamics*. Overland Park, Kansas: Globecom, 1984.

Shaw, Arnold. *Dictionary of American Pop/Rock*. New York: Schirmer, 1982.

———*The Rockin' Fifties*. New York: Hawthorn, 1975.

Shepherd, John. *Tin Pan Alley*. London: Routledge & Kegan Paul, 1982.

Sklar, Rick. *Rocking America*. New York: St. Martin's, 1984.

Smith, Wes. *The Pied Pipers of Rock 'n' Roll—Radio Deejays of the 50's and 60's*. Marietta, Georgia: Longstreet, 1989.

Solomon, Barbara (editor). *Ain't We Got Fun*. New York: New American Library, 1980.

Sterling, Christopher H. and John M. Kittross. *Stay Tuned* (second edition), Belmont, California: Wadsworth, 1990.

Stern, Michael and Jane. *Sixties People*. New York: Knopf, 1990.

Tosches, Nick. *Country*. New York: Charles Scribner's Sons, 1985.

Wenzel, Lynn and Carol J. Binkowski. *I Hear America Singing*. New York: Crown, 1989.

Whetmore, Edward Jay. *The Magic Medium: An Introduction to Radio in America*. Belmont, California: Wadsworth, 1981.

Whitburn, Joel (editor). *Pop Singles Annual*. Menomonee Falls, Wisconsin: Record Research, 1987.

Dlissertations

Linton, Bruce. "History of Chicago Radio Station Programming, 1921–31." Northwestern University, 1953.

Turnage, Joseph. "From Tin Pan Alley to Rock: Musical Transitions of the 1930's and 40's." Sonoma State University, 1986.

Articles

Numerous issues of *Record World* from 1970-75, and *Billboard Magazine* from the 1950s and 1960s were used in the process of writing this book.

Anson, Robert Sam. "Citizen Wenner. Part 1: The Rock Years." *New Times*, November 26, 1976, pp. 16–52.

Coase, R.H. "Payola in Radio and Televison Broadcasting." *Journal of Law and Economics*, University of Chicago Law School. Volume 22, #2, 1979, pp. 269–328.

Kinosian, Mike. "MD's: More than Music Librarians." *Radio & Records*, July 29, 1988, p. 70.

Lieberman, David. "The Sound of Money." *Business Week*, August 15, 1988, pp. 86–90. (A good study of the music business in the 1980s.)

Norberg, Eric. "What Turned FM Around." *The Gavin Report*, January 19, 1990, p. 23.

Tosches, Nick. "Ain't Nothin' but a Dance Wave: The Juggy Gayles Story." *WaxPaper* (Warner Brothers Records Magazine), February 9, 1979, pp. 9–11, 34–35.

Wilson, Earl. "The Song Pluggers at Work." *Liberty Magazine*, October 16, 1943, pp. 18–19, 53.

Other Publications

CBC: A Brief History of the Canadian Broadcasting Corporation. CBC Ottawa, 1976.

Facsimile edition of the first issue of *Variety* Magazine, December 16, 1905.

"Radio & Records: The First 15 Years." *Radio & Records*, Los Angeles, 1988.

Reymer & Gersin. "Radio Wars." National Assocation of Broadcasters, Washington, DC, 1983.

WTIC Radio: "60 Year Anniversary Tribute." WTIC Publications, Hartford, 1985.